Hedge Fund of Funds Investing

Other books by
Joseph G. Nicholas

Investing in Hedge Funds:
Strategies for the New Marketplace

Market-Neutral Investing:
Long/Short Hedge Fund Strategies

Also available from
Bloomberg Press

New Insights in Covered Call Writing:
The Powerful Technique That Enhances Return and
Lowers Risk in Stock Investing
by Richard Lehman and Lawrence G. McMillan

New Thinking in Technical Analysis:
Trading Models from the Masters
Edited by Rick Bensignor

Tom Dorsey's Trading Tips:
A Playbook for Stock Market Success
by Thomas J. Dorsey and the DWA Analysts

A complete list of our titles is available at
www.bloomberg.com/books

BLOOMBERG PROFESSIONAL LIBRARY

Hedge Fund of Funds Investing

An Investor's Guide

JOSEPH G. NICHOLAS

Bloomberg PRESS

PRINCETON

This publication contains the author's opinions and is designed to provide accurate and authoritative information. It is sold with the understanding that the author, publisher, and Bloomberg L.P. are not engaged in rendering legal, accounting, investment planning, business management, or other professional advice. The reader should seek the services of a qualified professional for such advice; the author, publisher, and Bloomberg L.P. cannot be held responsible for any loss incurred as a result of specific investments or planning decisions made by the reader.

First edition published 2004
1 3 5 7 9 10 8 6 4 2

Library of Congress Cataloging-in-Publication Data

Nicholas, Joseph G.
    Hedge fund of funds investing : an investor's guide / Joseph G. Nicholas. -- 1st ed.
        p. cm.
Includes index.
    ISBN 1-57660-124-2 (alk. paper)
  1. Hedge funds. I. Title.

    HG4530 .N53 2004
    332.64 '57--dc22   2003020939

Acquired and edited by Kathleen A. Peterson

To the memory of
Mary Sandretto Lizzadro

Contents

Part 2 HISTORICAL PERFORMANCE OF FUNDS OF FUNDS

Part 3   A COMMONSENSE APPROACH TO SELECTING FUNDS OF FUNDS

Acknowledgments

I THANK THE FOLLOWING:

For his contribution to all aspects of the book: Ben Borton.

For their insightful reading of and editorial contribution to the manuscript: Robert M. Pine, John Nicholas, and John Klimek.

For his work on charts, graphs, and related commentary: Dmitri Alexeev.

For his research contributions in the early stages: Barry Higgins.

For their help in building and improving the Hedge Fund Research database: all present and former employees of Hedge Fund Research, Inc.

For their stylistic and editorial recommendations: Kathleen Peterson and the staff at Bloomberg Press.

Introduction

Visions of wealth and exclusivity conjured by hedge funds have captured the imagination of investors for many years. Bold wagers taken with large sums of capital, rumors of fortunes gained and lost, global markets and even sovereign nations shaken by extremes of overleveraged finance—all are part of hedge fund mythology, but not indicative of the reality of hedge funds available to investors.

The aim of this book is to get beyond the hazy popular conceptions of hedge funds and to familiarize the prospective investor with the fundamentals of investing in hedge funds through what is called a fund of funds (FOF), an entity that pools capital from multiple investors and invests in two or more hedge funds.

Hedge funds have rightly gained the attention of private and institutional investors in recent years, given their strong absolute and risk-adjusted performance in general since 1990 and in particular when compared with equities since March 2000. Some of the doubts concerning hedge funds have been dispelled as hedge fund strategies performed admirably during the postbubble collapse of global equity markets. Hedge funds proved themselves as useful portfolio diversifiers and preservers of wealth. Talk of hedge funds as "risky" investments has waned as investors have come to realize that hedge funds generally have been a significantly less risky investment than a diversified portfolio of common stocks.

The potential benefits of including hedge funds in an investment portfolio are now clear: During the past few years of market declines and extreme stock volatility, hedge funds have held their value and generated positive returns. From January 1990 through December 2002, hedge funds returned 483 percent, outperforming the S&P 500 by 252 percent. Those who included hedge funds in their investment portfolios during this time significantly outperformed traditional long equity allocations. These lead investors have been followed by a multitude seeking the wealth preservation and diversification benefits of hedge funds.

Figure I-1   Return Versus Volatility, January 1990–December 2002

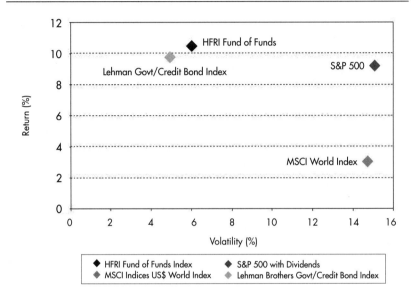

THE FUND OF FUNDS ADVANTAGE

An investor attempting to navigate in the field of hedge funds faces significant challenges: the large number of hedge funds, the diversity of strategies used, the range of financial instruments traded, and the various formats for investing in hedge funds. The fund of funds provides a ready solution to many of the complexities of investing in the unique set of investment strategies that collectively are referred to as hedge funds.

The fund of funds is a pooled vehicle for investing in multiple hedge funds. As with other investments, the goal of the investor in making a fund of funds investment is to match capital with appropriate investment opportunities.

Fund of funds managers are experts in hedge fund manager selection and asset allocation. Generally, a fund of funds will be managed by a team of professionals dedicated to researching underlying strategies and managers in an effort to assess the best investment opportunities. Given the large pool of hedge fund managers, the fund of funds manager needs to be able to efficiently collect and analyze hedge fund data and make investment choices that produce consistent, superior risk-adjusted returns. Since hedge funds are private investment vehicles that are not required to disclose information, this specialized expertise is vital to the fund of funds investment process.

The fund of funds, then, allows investors access to an attractive class of investments without necessitating that investors themselves develop the specialized knowledge required to prudently select individual hedge funds. What constitutes a fund of funds, how they operate, the benefits and risks of investing in one, and what to look for when deciding to invest in a fund of funds are the subject matter of this book.

THE STRUCTURE OF THIS BOOK

In my first book, *Investing in Hedge Funds*, I addressed the hedge fund industry in general and presented an overview of the various strategies pursued by hedge fund managers. My second book, *Market-Neutral Investing*, analyzed the facets of long/short hedge fund strategy in more detail. This book, the third in the series, discusses the increasingly important fund of hedge funds investing format, a pooled investment vehicle that offers combinations of different hedge fund strategies and managers.

The goal of this book is to provide investors who are new to the hedge fund industry with a practical guide to understanding and evaluating funds of funds. Basic industry concepts are introduced and their importance discussed based on my experience both as an observer and manager of funds of funds. As with any specialized field, the fund of funds industry has its own vocabulary and jargon. With that in mind, I have made an effort to identify and define these specialized terms throughout the text.

In an attempt to create a useful resource for investors considering a fund of funds investment, I have organized the book into three parts. Part 1 provides an overview of the fund of funds industry:

■ *Fund of funds* defined
■ Options for investing in hedge funds
■ Changes in the hedge fund industry
■ Hedge fund and fund of funds structures
■ The mechanics of fund of funds investing
■ The benefits and risks of fund of funds investing

Part 2, which focuses on fund of funds performance, presents an analysis of fund of funds historical performance. It also discusses performance expectations for adding funds of funds to a portfolio of traditional assets.

If investing in a fund of funds is determined to be the appropriate mode of accessing hedge fund returns, a plan is needed for sifting through the many available choices. Part 3 of this book lays out a framework for evaluating and selecting a fund of funds that is appropriate for the investor's needs. The process can be broken down into four steps:

1 Defining objectives and parameters
2 Screening to create a fund of funds short list
3 Conducting general due diligence on the short list
4 Evaluating finalists for selection

Chapter 7, covering Steps 1 and 2, discusses setting investment objectives and parameters and screening through the fund of funds universe for an appropriate short list of candidates for more in-depth due diligence. Due diligence consists of gathering all available information, confirming verifiable aspects (such as a manager's professional degrees, regulatory history), and importantly, performing extensive and detailed evaluation of this information. Areas of review include the portfolio management's expertise, the abilities of the firm, the investment structure, risk management, and fund performance. Documents to be reviewed include the due diligence questionnaire, offering memorandum, responses to marketing materials, fund documentation, the subscription agreement, and any other documents that may be available for scrutiny such as the firm Form ADV filed with the Securities and Exchange Commission. Chapters 8–10 explore in greater detail Step 3, the due diligence process.

As a framework, the questions recommended in the standardized due diligence questionnaire provided by the Alternative Investment Management Association (AIMA) are used.[1] A summary accompanies each group of questions, followed by insights into potential answers to each specific question.

Chapter 8 looks at the fund of funds firm as a business concern; Chapter 9 discusses the portfolio management capabilities of the fund of funds firm, including asset allocation and manager selection; and Chapter 10 explains the risk management capabilities of the fund of funds firm. Finally, in Chapter 11, a case study is provided covering Step 4, which evaluates fund of funds finalists for selection.

I am as excited about existing and future opportunities in hedge funds as I was in the late 1980s when I first entered the industry. It is global in scope and captures the best in entrepreneurial intellect and investment talent. The growth of hedge funds, due to superior performance and a diverse set of investment approaches, reflects the unabated human pursuit of opportunity. As with most prospects for profit, however, they go hand in hand with risk. Investors need to understand both sides of the coin in their pursuit of investment returns. My hope is that this book will assist them in better understanding the potential risks and rewards of investing in hedge funds through funds of funds.

Note

1. The full AIMA questionnaire "AIMA Illustrative Questionnaire for Due Diligence of Fund of Funds Managers" can be found in Appendix A.

PART 1

The

Fund of Funds

Industry

Fund of Funds in the Hedge Fund Industry *1*

A FUND OF FUNDS (FOF) is a fund *whose investment strategy is to allocate capital to two or more hedge funds.* Investors purchase an interest in a fund of funds, and their assets are commingled with those of other investors. This pool of money is invested with a number of hedge funds. The basic structure is diagramed in *Figure 1-1.*

It is estimated that there are more than nine hundred funds of funds in operation today, and there are many more being developed. As a group, they represent more than one-third of assets invested in hedge funds.

For most investors, the fund of funds provide an efficient and

Figure 1-1 Fund of Funds Structure

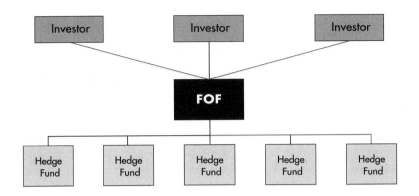

cost-effective way to invest. It spares them the task of having to select and gain access to suitable hedge fund managers from the ever-
expanding universe of investment possibilities. It also improves
their chance of investing in hedge funds successfully, which requires, as with most successful investments, considerable resources,
experience, and time. For investors with smaller assets to invest, a
fund of funds provides access to a diversified group of hedge funds
that could not be achieved directly due to minimum investment
requirements. The private nature of the hedge fund industry—
in most cases there is no requirement for hedge funds to publicly
disclose information—creates a situation in which experienced
firms focusing resources on this investment area can build a significant and sustainable informational advantage that allows them to
add value for their investors.

Hedge Fund Investment Options

The decision to allocate capital to hedge funds is based on an evaluation of the merits of the investment opportunities presented by
the underlying strategies (for detailed summaries of the strategies
and performance achieved, see Chapter 2). Over the past ten years
hedge fund strategies have produced compelling risk-adjusted returns on an absolute basis as well as positive diversification benefits

when combined with a portfolio of traditional assets. However, the decision to make an investment in hedge funds is only the first step in a multitiered process. Investors must then determine the most appropriate vehicle for accessing hedge fund strategies. This second point presents a hedge fund investor with a number of potential difficulties: with which strategies and which managers should they invest, how much capital should be dedicated, how is the structural risk associated with hedge fund investments controlled, and how will the investments be monitored?

A number of investment options are available. The four principle options are: (1) investing directly in a single hedge fund, (2) building a customized portfolio that combines a number of hedge funds, (3) investing through an index fund, and (4) investing in a fund of funds.

DIRECT INVESTMENT

One approach is for investors to make direct investments into hedge funds they select. Investment minimums for hedge funds, that is, the minimum amount required to invest with a manager, typically range from half a million to several million dollars. Investing directly, therefore, requires significant assets if an investor wants good diversification by manager and strategy. Investing in one or a handful of managers increases the burden of manager selection and increases the risk of substandard performance results because of the concentration of investment.

CUSTOMIZED PORTFOLIO

A second method of direct investment is to create a customized portfolio of hedge funds managed specifically to meet the needs of the investor. The portfolio follows a fund of funds investment strategy, but does not accept outside capital; it is managed internally, either by the investor or in conjunction with an outside investment adviser or consultant. This approach requires the same investment expertise as managing a fund of funds. Because of the cost of hiring experienced investment professionals, plus the expense of legal, accounting, and administration, this is a solution best suited for a large-scale investor who has the resources and commitment to maintain the ongoing analyses and due diligence necessary to prudently manage a fund of funds.

INDEX FUND

A third way to invest in hedge funds is to access the hedge fund industry or specific strategy returns by investing through an investable hedge fund index. Investing in an index is more cost effective than other approaches and is available to both individual and institutional investors. The goal of the index is to deliver the market return of the hedge fund industry or that of one of its underlying strategies. Unlike a fund of funds, such an index is not actively managed but follows an allocation methodology designed to mimic the collective exposures of the greater hedge fund industry.

FUND OF FUNDS INVESTMENT

The fourth approach is to invest in an existing fund of funds. Funds of funds can provide an efficient solution to the challenge of investing in hedge funds. Indeed, they have become the most common means of access for investors who are looking for diversified exposure to hedge funds, but who do not have the resources to research, monitor, and manage multiple hedge funds. For many investors desiring access to hedge fund returns, investing in a fund of funds is an obvious choice. It should come as no surprise, then, that the absolute number and total assets flowing into fund of funds vehicles have contributed greatly to the rapid growth of the hedge fund industry.

GROWTH OF FUNDS OF FUNDS

The equity culture that reached its apex during the bull market of the late 1990s has been reevaluated, given the sharp losses suffered by investors since the early years of the new millennium. World

Figure 1-2 Growth of Fund of Funds (FOF) Assets by Billions of Dollars

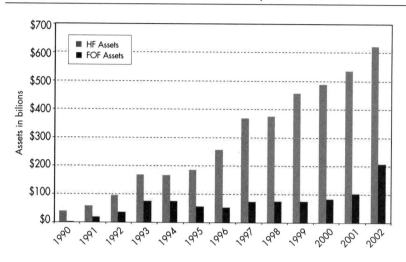

Figure 1-3 Growth of Fund of Funds (FOF) Assets by Percentage

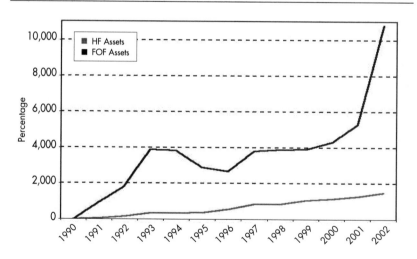

markets have worked through the excesses of that technology-led bubble. The ensuing recession in the United States, and the realization that equity market returns can remain subdued for an extended period of time, have resulted in investors looking elsewhere for attractive returns that are not dependent on the direction of the equity markets.

Hedge funds possess both of these qualities and, as one might expect, have received substantial asset flows as a result. The number of funds of funds and the assets controlled by these investment vehicles have grown apace. The annual growth rate for fund of funds assets since 1990 has been 48 percent. This compares to an average annual asset growth rate for the hedge fund industry as a whole of 26 percent. The graphs in *Figures 1-2* and *1-3* show that fund of funds growth has actually outpaced hedge fund industry growth. While the industry as a whole is quite young, the fund of funds industry is younger still. In fact, as shown in *Figure 1-4*, more than 75 percent of funds of funds in existence today were started since 1996, and less than 10 percent were in existence in 1990.

Figure 1-4 Fund of Funds Distribution by Inception Year

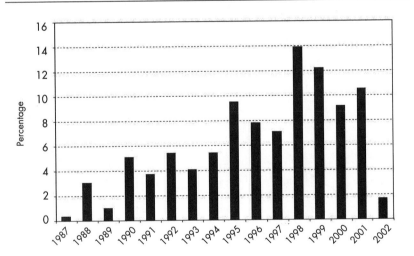

Outlined below are the seven most important factors contributing to the rapid growth in both the number of funds of funds and assets in funds of funds.

1 **Viability of hedge fund strategies/acceptance of hedge funds.** Attracted by the performance-based compensation (which averages about 1.5 percent of assets and 20 percent of profits annually), innovative and flexible strategies, and increasing investor demand, many of the best and brightest minds in the asset management industry have started hedge funds in the past five years. Rapid acceptance of and investment in hedge funds, however, has also drawn in managers who are less seasoned and less experienced in hedge fund strategies and techniques. This proliferation of funds has made the challenging task of selecting appropriate managers even more onerous. As previously noted and discussed in detail later, the fund of funds allows an investor to outsource the responsibility of manager selection and strategy allocation to a team of experienced professionals dedicated full time to the project.

2 **Informational advantage.** The private nature of the hedge fund industry means that information is not equally distributed among all participants. Funds of funds, however, seek to gain an edge by creating databases of fund information and collating data gleaned from various channels, such as data providers, prime brokers, and industry contacts. Some of this information is available to the fund of funds only because of its position as an asset allocator. The ability of funds of funds to access, collect, and interpret data essential to successful hedge fund investing has been and will continue to be a key driver of their growth.

3 **Special access to closed funds.** Successful hedge funds may close to new investment in order to preserve their ability to implement their investment strategy. However, funds of funds, as existing investors, often enter into arrangements with favored managers to reserve a certain amount of capacity in the event that the manager's fund becomes closed to

new investment. In this way, fund of funds investors may have access to successful funds closed to new investment. Even if no additional capacity remains, a fund of funds investor still participates in the existing exposure in the closed manager.

4 Economies of scale. By pooling investor capital, funds of funds achieve economies of scale. Investing in hedge funds requires high minimums, and the work necessary to perform due diligence and select managers, conduct risk management, and administer multiple investments is costly. Funds of funds help individual investors circumvent problems associated with minimum investment sizes, and share the costs associated with the research-intensive manager selection process, reporting, and aggregating information from multiple hedge fund sources. Therefore, the pooling of capital allows smaller investors a superior and more efficient way to invest in multiple hedge funds.

5 Educational role. As part of its sales efforts, a fund of funds educates investors about the risks and merits of hedge fund strategies and how different performance objectives can be achieved depending on how strategies and managers are combined and managed in a fund of funds portfolio. Many first-time hedge fund investors look to funds of funds not simply as an investment vehicle, but as a way of learning about hedge fund strategies and hedge fund managers along with how they should be selected for incorporation into multiple manager allocations.

6 Diversification. For investors looking to make a representative investment in hedge funds, diversified funds of funds are an obvious choice. By adding more managers, the risk that is specific to any particular manager is reduced. Additionally, some funds of funds seek to achieve defined diversification goals across strategies and substrategies to avoid the risks of having managers taking similar market risk.

7 Performance. Even with all the other factors, funds of funds would not grow without generating good performance. Investors, in general, look to funds of funds to produce attractive absolute returns relative to other investment options and to produce returns above that of the hedge fund industry.

HEDGE FUND INDUSTRY CHARACTERISTICS AND TRENDS

Before examining the fund of funds approach to investing in hedge funds, it is essential to first understand the hedge fund industry and the fund of funds' place in that industry.

There are two key aspects of the hedge fund industry to observe:

1 The hedge fund industry consists of a number of different investment strategies.
2 The investment strategies are dynamic, and the percentage of industry investment allocated to each strategy has changed significantly over the past decade.

To understand hedge funds is to understand the variety of investment approaches used by hedge fund managers. Each strategy consists of a number of substrategies or variations on the core investment theme. In Chapter 2, we examine the underlying hedge fund strategies in greater detail. For now, it is important to note that the number, type, and asset size of the strategies and substrategies shift over time, influenced by changes in market conditions, increasing or decreasing opportunities and inefficiencies, and changes in investor demand for return characteristics. The strategies that make up the industry today are not the same as in the past and are likely to be different in the future.

During the 1990s, rapid gains in technology leveled the financial playing field and allowed investment managers to leave their employment at large investment houses and start their own firms. In addition, the bull market gave these managers a great financial incentive to do so. Large asset flows into equities particularly supported the growth in equity-oriented hedge funds. Consider the

Figure 1-5 Strategy Composition Within Hedge Fund Industry
by Assets Under Management: 1990

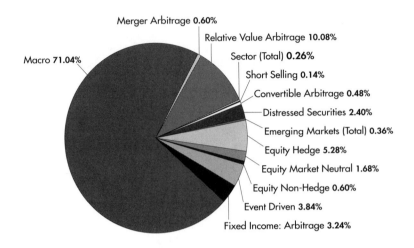

graphs in *Figures 1-5* and *1-6*, which show the composition of hedge fund strategies in 1990 and 2002, respectively. During this period, the strategy weights of the hedge fund industry shifted quite dramatically. For example, as increased information flow and efficiency in global markets reduced traditional opportunities for macro investing, the stock market expansion of the 1990s created a broader base for equity opportunities. Note the reduction of industry assets in the so-called Macro strategy allocating from 71 percent in 1990 to 13 percent in 2002, and the corresponding growth in Equity Hedge from 5 percent in 1990 to 30 percent in 2002. (See *Figure 1-7.*)

These long-term trends in strategy allocations are driven by market conditions and investor preferences. For example, consider the first quarter of 2002. During this period, the major beneficiaries of asset flows were Distressed Securities and Event Driven strategies. The opportunity in the distressed arena had expanded dramatically as default rates increased over the prior two years. These flows suggest that investors perceived that this strategy would achieve superior returns. The largest outflow in the first quarter of 2002 was

Figure 1-6 Strategy Composition Within Hedge Fund Industry
by Assets Under Management: 2002

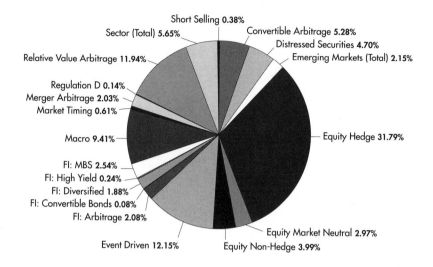

Figure 1-7 Selected Strategies as a Percentage of Total Hedge Fund Assets

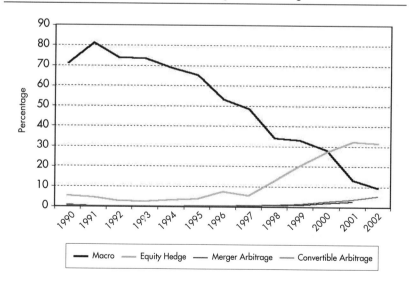

Figure 1-8 Estimated Strategy Inflow/Outflow: 1Q 2002

Strategy	Inflow	Outflow
Convertible Arbitrage	$495.80	
Distressed Securities	$592.62	
Emerging Markets (Total)	$374.63	
Equity Hedge	$498.74	
Equity Market Neutral		($88.91)
Equity Non-Hedge		($21.66)
Event Driven	$518.11	
Fixed Income: Arbitrage	$125.07	
Fixed Income: Convertible Bonds	$0.22	
Fixed Income: Diversified		($22.17)
Fixed Income: High Yield	$69.80	
Fixed Income: Mortgage-Backed		($1.05)
Macro	$412.61	
Market Timing	$36.34	
Merger Arbitrage		($394.22)
Regulation D		($212.51)
Relative Value Arbitrage (RVA)	$659.03	
Sector (Total)	$112.80	
Short Selling		($48.84)
Statistical Arbitrage		($32.83)
Total Inflow/Outflow	**$3,895.76**	**($822.20)**
Net Inflow	**$3,073.57**	

from Merger Arbitrage. In stark contrast to the distressed arena, merger deal flow plummeted over the previous twelve months, and returns to the strategy moderated accordingly. This perceived lack of opportunity caused investors to shift assets away from the strategy. *Figure 1-8* shows complete details of first quarter fund flows for the twenty principal hedge fund strategies.

HEDGE FUND INVESTMENT STRUCTURE

Today the term *hedge fund* is a generic label for all of the diverse strategies used by hedge fund managers. The term itself is said to have been coined to describe what Alfred Winslow Jones did in 1949 when he combined a leveraged long stock position with a portfolio of short stocks in an investment fund with an incentive fee structure. Since then, the scope of the term *hedge fund* has expanded beyond this specific strategy (a leveraged long portfolio "hedged" by short stock sales) to describe funds engaging in a range of investment strategies. The commonality of these funds is their commingled investment structure, typically a limited partnership or offshore corporation. Like the term *mutual fund*, which describes only the investment structure and does not indicate whether the fund invests in stocks or bonds or in the United States or abroad, the term *hedge fund* does not tell an investor anything about the underlying investment activities. Thus, a hedge fund acts as a vehicle within which one or more of the investment strategies described in Chapter 2 are pursued.

It should be noted that hedge funds differ from traditional mutual funds in the range of allowable investment approaches, the goals of the strategies they use, their typically private nature (they do not have to be registered with a regulatory agency such as the Securities and Exchange Commission), methodology of manager compensation (management fee plus an incentive or performance fee), breadth of financial instruments traded, and range of investment techniques employed. This distinction, however, is becoming blurred as mutual fund regulatory changes and investor demand have allowed certain hedge fund strategies to operate under the mutual fund structure.

Since the term *hedge fund* describes an investment structure and has been applied to a range of strategies, in order to understand particular hedge funds it is necessary to separate the structure of the investment (its legal form and method of operations) from its investment strategy (how it invests capital in the financial markets to achieve its goals).

The *investment structure* is the legal entity that allows investment assets to be pooled and permits the hedge fund manager to invest them. The *investment approach* the manager takes is known as the hedge fund strategy or alternative investment strategy. The structure establishes such things as how manager compensation is determined; how many investors he or she can accept; the type of investor allowed to invest in the hedge fund; and what the investors' rights are related to profits, taxes, and reports. The elements that make up the strategy include how the manager will invest, the markets and instruments that will be used, and the opportunity and return source that will be targeted.

LEGAL STRUCTURE

Hedge funds and funds of funds have very similar investment structures. These come in a variety of legal forms depending on where they are located and the type of investor the fund organizer wishes to attract. To avoid entity-level tax, in the United States they are usually formed as limited partnerships, or in some cases, limited liability companies or trusts.

Limited partnerships are organized under state law (for example, as an Illinois Limited Partnership). The general form is not unique to hedge funds but rather is used for various businesses. A limited partnership has one or more general partners and a number of limited partners. The general partner can be an individual or a corporation and is responsible for the management and operation of the partnership and has unlimited liability. The manager will typically be the general partner but act through an entity to avoid unlimited personal liability for fund obligations.

The limited partners have liability "limited" to the amount they invest or "pay" for their limited partnership interests. Generally, they are allocated a pro rata share of all investments and expenses of the fund. The limited partnership interests are not traded and cannot be sold to any other prospective investor. They can be sold back to the partnership or "redeemed" only under the procedures established in the partnership agreement.

Offshore funds present a second legal form. Offshore funds are funds organized outside of the United States, usually in an offshore tax haven such as the Cayman Islands, Bermuda, the British Virgin Islands, and the Bahamas. Typically, a corporate structure is used, but because of the tax haven, no entity-level tax is imposed. Instead of a general partner, these structures have a management company. Investors purchase shares, and, as is the case with domestic funds, their liability is limited to the amount they invest. For tax reasons, offshore funds typically are comprised primarily of non-U.S. investors. However, many managers of offshore funds permit tax-exempt U.S. investors, such as pension plans, endowments, and charitable trusts, to participate. Sometimes, fund managers create both a domestic fund and a parallel offshore fund. In that case, the manager may offer one or both options to tax-exempt investors. (Sometimes, the manager will prefer to keep all tax-exempt investors in the offshore fund, in order to avoid using up participant openings, or "slots.")

NUMBERS OF INVESTORS AND MINIMUM INVESTMENT SIZE

Hedge funds and funds of funds are usually private investment vehicles. In the United States this means that under one of the available exemptions the securities that hedge funds offer to investors (the limited partnership or limited liability company interests) need not be registered with the Securities and Exchange Commission (SEC) to be offered to the public. The exemptions specify certain requirements in order to avoid registration. These generally deal with the type of investor allowed to invest in the fund, the number of investors that can invest (the previously mentioned "slots"), and how the investors can be solicited. Most U.S. state securities laws (blue sky laws) also contain exemptions from registration for limited or private offerings.

In addition, hedge funds and funds of funds structure the investment vehicle to fall within one of the several exemptions from SEC registration provided in the Investment Company Act of 1940, as amended. Until 1997, the most common exemption that was followed, known as 3(c)(1), limited participants to ninety-nine investors. In 1997, under the National Securities Markets Improvements Act (NSMIA), a further exemption, known as 3(c)(7), was enacted. It created a new exclusion from the definition of an "investment company" for investment pools if all investors are "qualified purchasers" with no limit on the number of investors. A qualified purchaser is

1 an individual holding at least $5,000,000 in investments;
2 a family company that owns not less than $5,000,000 in investments;
3 a person, acting for its, his, or her own account or for the accounts of other qualified purchasers, who owns and invests on a discretionary basis at least $25,000,000 in investments;
4 a company, regardless of the amount of such company's investment(s), if each beneficial owner of the company's securities is a qualified purchaser;
5 a trust if each of the trustee(s) and settlor(s) is a qualified purchaser.

Both the 3(c)(1) and 3(c)(7) exemptions require that the sale of securities not be made by way of a public offering.

Because the exemptions from registration often limit the number of investors or require that investors meet certain standards, hedge funds and funds of funds usually require large minimum investments. The minimum investment size ranges from $100,000 to $10 million, but usually is in the $500,000 to $1 million range. Minimums are usually larger onshore where limits apply to U.S. investors.

In the early stages, when a hedge fund has few investors and is trying to raise funds, it tends to have lower minimums and more flexibility to waive the minimum and accept a lesser amount. As the number of investors in the fund increases, the remaining slots become more valuable, and managers are less likely to waive the minimum. In many cases, the fund actually raises the minimum for new investors and in some cases kicks out the smaller players to make room for larger allocations. Because of the more limited asset capacity of many of the hedge fund strategies, many managers also limit the size of any individual investment to ensure a diversified client base.

The minimum investment restrictions mean that building a diversified portfolio of hedge fund investments requires considerable capital. By pooling the capital of like-minded investors seeking to access multiple hedge funds, the fund of fund can offer a single minimum investment far below that of the underlying hedge funds.

REPORTING AND DISCLOSURE

Hedge funds and funds of funds have historically calculated and reported performance on a monthly or quarterly basis. The level of fund of funds reporting is dependent on the information provided by the underlying hedge funds. In response to increased investor demand, some funds now report weekly, and even daily, estimates, but the industry as a whole normally provides monthly performance results. Furthermore, there is no standard reporting format. Some hedge funds provide faxes of percentage profit or loss. Others send detailed statements to each investor with a letter describing the fund's investment activities and results. Most managers, however, provide monthly returns for the previous period within two weeks by fax, mail, or e-mail. Audits and the K1s (partner tax statements) are sent to investors annually. Like all hedge fund investors, funds of funds, except for those that invest in separately managed accounts, are dependent on underlying managers for performance reporting, and because these individual results must be consolidated into a report for the fund of funds, its report generally will not be available until the end of the second week of the following month.

Reporting of portfolio exposure information is less uniform than performance reporting, with practices ranging from no disclosure to full position transparency. The trend is clearly toward more transparency, with managers increasingly making at least summary exposure information available for their funds. An important function of the fund of funds manager is to collect and aggregate exposure information from all underlying managers and make assessments of the aggregate exposure of the fund of funds.

LIQUIDITY

In a hedge fund context, liquidity refers to the timing and notice period required for investors to redeem their investment and have their money returned from the fund. For example, quarterly liquidity means that an investor can take money out of the funds at the end of each calendar quarter, while monthly liquidity means that an investor can get out at the end of each month. One mistake that many investors make is not factoring in the "notice period" they are required to give before they can redeem their investments. Some hedge funds cannot generate cash for investor redemptions on short notice and require notice periods that range from 30 to 90 days. For example, for a fund that allows redemption at the end of each calendar quarter and requires a 60-day notice, an investor wishing to redeem on June 30 must notify the fund in writing by April 30. An investor waiting until May to notify the fund cannot get out until September 30.

The redemption provisions also specify what time frame a fund has to actually pay the investor back in full. In the above example the fund might have 30 days to pay 90 percent of the investment. The remaining 10 percent is held back until the fund's year-end audit is completed, which may mean that final payment will be received by the investor in March or April of the following year. This holdover provision generally only applies to investors who redeem the full amount of their investment. Because funds of funds invest in hedge funds, they must provide liquidity based on what is available in the underlying hedge fund investments or have arrangements to borrow to cover the redemption timing difference.

Hedge funds may not be required to make payment in cash. Certain funds generally, and many funds in extreme circumstances such as liquidation, may make payment in securities rather than in cash. This is particularly true for funds holding private or illiquid securities, such as those of bankrupt companies. But it is not the case for all hedge funds, and some hedge fund managers make all efforts to accommodate investors by returning their capital as early as possible in cash. A fund's offering memorandum will specify its ability to make payments in cash or securities. Similarly, funds of funds may provide that they will redeem "in kind," that is, in the form of the underlying securities that they might receive from the underlying hedge funds.

LOCKUP

A lockup period is the length of time that investors must remain invested before their investment can be redeemed or becomes subject to the standard liquidity provision. The lockup period for hedge funds ranges from a few months to one or more years, but usually the lockup in U.S. funds is one year. It works like this: If the liquidity is quarterly and the lockup is one year, then an investor who invests on January 1 cannot redeem until December 31 of the same year. Once a year has passed, liquidity becomes quarterly, so the next date when a redemption would be allowed is March 31 of the following year.

The liquidity of underlying hedge funds will influence, if not determine, the liquidity provisions of a fund of funds. In order to meet its own redemptions, a fund of funds must redeem from the underlying funds in which it has invested in order to have cash available unless it arranges for borrowing to meet redemption demands.

SUMMARY

The fund of funds is perhaps the largest single investor type allocation to hedge funds. Of the various options available to investors for accessing the returns of hedge fund strategies, a fund of funds provides significant benefits and advantages, particularly where a diversified exposure to hedge funds is desired. Structurally, funds of funds have many similarities to hedge funds, their features being dependent on those of the underlying hedge fund investments.

WITH THESE BASIC INSIGHTS about hedge fund structures in place, we are ready to move on to a discussion of the underlying hedge fund strategies.

Hedge Fund Investment Strategies *2*

A LL HEDGE FUNDS are not the same. Although they appear to be so in structure, each hedge fund is unique when the investment it pursues is considered. In almost all cases, each hedge fund manager is a specialist pursuing a very specific investment approach called the investment style or strategy. Hedge funds can be grouped according to the general strategy pursued, but within such groupings multiple substrategies exist.

An investment strategy is an approach to selecting securities, or a portfolio of securities, based on an investment philosophy designed to derive returns by taking unique risks in the financial markets. For example, all merger arbitrageurs derive returns by taking long and short positions in companies engaged in a merger, thereby taking the "event risk" associated with the deal not going through. Hedge Fund Research, Inc. (HFR)[1] groups these hedge fund investment strategies into thirteen categories. Strategy groupings are determined by the core opportunity being accessed, the source of return, the risks taken, and the instruments used. Each category is further divided into subcategories. This more granular categorization allows for variations on core strategy themes. Only by examining funds and their managers at this substrategy level of detail is it possible to develop a meaningful understanding of the return potential and the associated risk.

What follows are brief summaries of the major hedge fund strategy categories. These descriptions are meant to be only a summary guide to the types of investment approaches being followed by the underlying hedge fund managers to which fund of funds (FOF) managers may allocate capital. For more in-depth descriptions of hedge fund strategies, see *Investing in Hedge Funds* and *Market-Neutral Investing.*[2]

Hedge fund strategies cover a wide range of return and risk characteristics. The table in *Figure 2-1* shows the major strategies by annualized rates of return and standard deviation to demonstrate the range of possible outcomes across strategies.

These summary statistics are based on performance indices calculated by HFR. The methodology used is to equally weight all funds in any given strategy that are currently reporting to the HFR database. Although the resultant index gives a good indication of what the strategy as a whole is offering at any given time, it may mask a wide dispersion of returns within the group. This is certainly the case in some of the more broadly defined categories such as Equity Hedge, Event Driven, and Macro (also known as Global Macro). The dispersion will be less in a more narrowly defined strategy such as Merger Arbitrage. The charts in *Figures 2-2* and *2-3* show the dispersion of quarterly returns in, respectively, a broadly defined strategy grouping (Equity Hedge) and a narrowly defined grouping

Figure 2-1 Principal Hedge Fund Strategies
           January 1990–December 2002

	Annualized Rate of Return	Annualized Standard Deviation	Sharpe Ratio	Maximum Drawdown
HFRI Convertible Arbitrage Index	11.64	3.38	1.81	4.84
HFRI Distressed Securities Index	14.33	6.36	1.36	12.78
HFRI Emerging Markets	13.46	15.73	0.57	43.37
HFRI Equity Hedge Index	18.18	9.36	1.31	10.30
HFRI Equity Market Neutral Index	10.30	3.28	1.50	2.72
HFRI Event Driven Index	14.24	6.87	1.25	10.78
HFRI Fixed Income	10.90	3.65	1.49	8.25
HFRI Fixed Income Arbitrage	8.58	4.62	0.73	14.42
HFRI Macro Index	16.84	8.76	1.26	10.70
HFRI Market Timing Index	13.16	6.94	1.10	5.50
HFRI Merger Arbitrage Index	11.13	4.48	1.27	6.32
HFRI Relative Value Arbitrage Index	13.06	3.80	1.95	6.55
HFRI Sector	19.27	14.40	0.97	34.30
HFRI Short Selling Index	3.71	22.76	0.05	53.36

Figure 2-2 Quarterly Performance Dispersion—Equity Hedge
           Q1 1992–Q4 2002

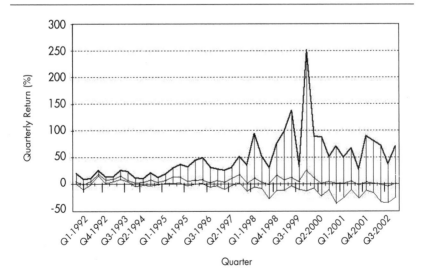

Figure 2-3 Quarterly Performance Dispersion—Merger Arbitrage
Q1 1992–Q4 2002

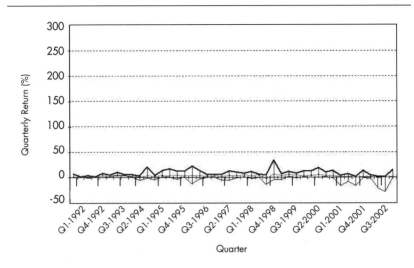

Figure 2-4 Comparative Strategy Performance
January 1990–December 2002

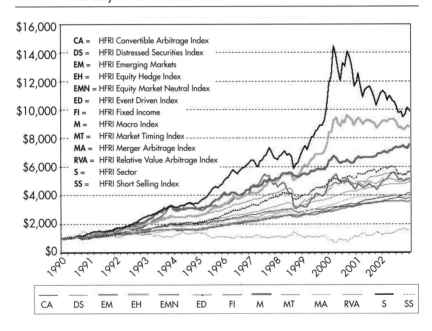

CA = HFRI Convertible Arbitrage Index
DS = HFRI Distressed Securities Index
EM = HFRI Emerging Markets
EH = HFRI Equity Hedge Index
EMN = HFRI Equity Market Neutral Index
ED = HFRI Event Driven Index
FI = HFRI Fixed Income
M = HFRI Macro Index
MT = HFRI Market Timing Index
MA = HFRI Merger Arbitrage Index
RVA = HFRI Relative Value Arbitrage Index
S = HFRI Sector
SS = HFRI Short Selling Index

(Merger Arbitrage). The greater the dispersion, the more important the role of the fund of funds manager in selecting managers.

The chart in *Figure 2-4* shows the comparative performance over time of the various hedge fund strategies.

CONVERTIBLE ARBITRAGE

Convertible Arbitrage involves taking a long security position and hedging market risk by taking offsetting positions, often in different securities, of the same issuer. A manager may, in an effort to capitalize on relative pricing inefficiencies, purchase long positions in convertible securities, generally convertible bonds or warrants, and hedge a portion of the equity risk by selling short the underlying common stock. A manager may also seek to hedge interest rate or credit exposure under some circumstances. For example, a manager can be long convertible bonds and short the underlying issuer's equity, and may also use futures to hedge out interest rate risk or credit default swaps to hedge default risk. Timing may be linked to a specific event relative to the underlying company, or a belief that a relative mispricing exists between the corresponding securities.

CONVERTIBLE ARBITRAGE SUBSTRATEGIES

A manager can choose to emphasize trades that generate income or those that depend on volatility for trading opportunities. A third area is "busted," or high yield, convertibles. This technique requires a great deal of credit analysis and derives a significant portion of return from the high yields on distressed convertibles. Because most convertible managers participate in different portions of the curve at different times, it is difficult to classify managers in one of these groups unless they explicitly specialize there. Most managers group into aggressive or conservative camps. Aggressive managers use higher levels of leverage, may not fully hedge their stock risk, or may have a higher concentration in one area—in all cases, making them subject to a higher-level interest rate, credit, or volatility risk than their peers.

Figure 2-5 Convertible Arbitrage Strategy Performance
            January 1990–December 2002

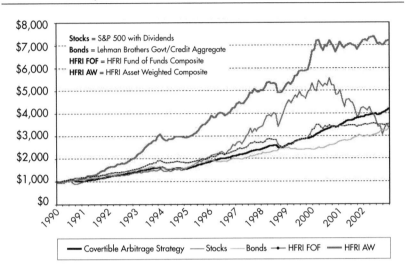

DISTRESSED SECURITIES

Distressed Securities managers both invest in and may sell short the securities of companies where the security's price has been or is expected to be affected by a distressed situation. A *distressed security* may be defined as a security or other obligation of a company that is encountering significant financial or business difficulties, including companies that (1) may be engaged in debt restructuring or other capital transactions of a similar nature while outside the jurisdiction of federal bankruptcy law, (2) are subject to the provisions of federal bankruptcy law, or (3) are experiencing poor operating results due to unfavorable operating conditions, overleveraged capital structure, catastrophic events, extraordinary write-offs, or special competitive or product obsolescence problems. These managers seek profit opportunities arising from inefficiencies in the market for such securities and other obligations.

Negative events, and the subsequent announcement of a proposed restructuring or reorganization to address the problem, may

Figure 2-6 Distressed Securities Strategy Performance
January 1990–December 2002

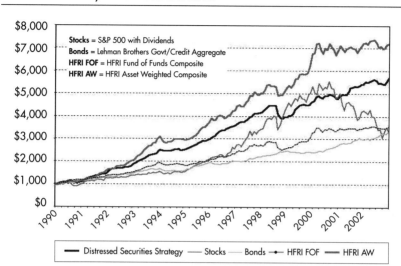

create a severe market imbalance as some holders attempt to sell their positions at a time when few investors are willing to purchase the securities or other obligations of the troubled company. If a manager believes that a market imbalance exists and the securities and other obligations of the troubled company may be purchased at prices below their value, he may purchase them. Increasingly, Distressed Securities managers have looked to complement long positions with short positions in companies headed for financial distress. Profits in this sector result from the market's lack of understanding of the true value of the deeply discounted securities as well as mispricings within a distressed company's capital structure.

DISTRESSED SECURITIES SUBSTRATEGIES

Within the Distressed Securities category there are two primary substrategies. The first, Deep Value, involves an extremely long-biased buy-and-hold strategy, in which a manager takes significant positions in a distressed company and may take an active role in the workout. Risk levels within the category are determined by the use of leverage, position concentration, and liquidity of the underlying investments.

With the Long/Short substrategy, managers hold a balance between long and short positions in distressed companies. These positions often take the form of capital structure arbitrage, that is, long and short positions in different securities of the same company when those securities are mispriced relative to one another. Risk levels within the category are determined by the use of leverage, position concentration, and liquidity of the underlying investments.

EMERGING MARKETS

Emerging Markets strategies involve primarily long investments in the securities of companies in countries with developing, or "emerging," financial markets. Managers make particular use of specialized knowledge and an on-the-ground presence in markets where financial information is often scarce. Such knowledge and presence creates an informational edge that allows them to take advantage of mispricings caused by emerging market inefficiencies. They make profits by mining these markets for undervalued assets and purchasing them before the market corrects itself. Because of the less developed and less liquid nature of these markets, emerging markets securities are generally more volatile than securities traded in developed markets. Managers can be differentiated by country exposures and types of instruments utilized.

EMERGING MARKETS SUBSTRATEGIES

Primarily distinguished by geographical orientation, Emerging Markets substrategies include Asia, Eastern Europe, Latin America, or Global. Risk levels are determined by position concentration, liquidity of the underlying investments, and the types of securities being traded. All emerging market investments are volatile, but dollar- or euro-denominated debt is usually less so than local currency bonds and equities.

Figure 2-7   Emerging Markets Strategy Performance
January 1990–December 2002

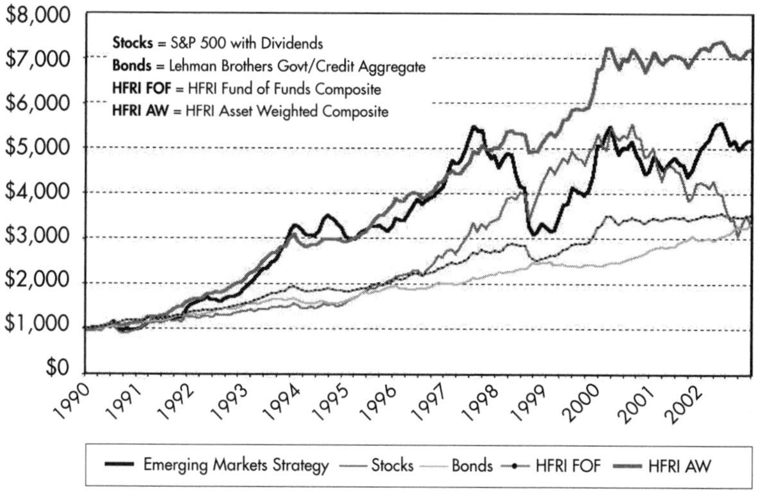

EQUITY HEDGE

Equity Hedge, also known as Long/Short Equity, combines core long holdings of equities with short sales of stock, stock indices, or derivatives related to equity markets. Net exposure of Equity Hedge portfolios may range anywhere from net long to net short, depending on market conditions. Managers generally increase net long exposure in bull markets and decrease net long exposure (or may even be net short) in bear markets. Generally, the short exposure is intended to generate an ongoing positive return in addition to acting as a hedge against a general stock market decline. Stock index put options or exchange-traded funds are also often used as a hedge against market risk.

In a rising market, Equity Hedge managers expect their long holdings to appreciate more than the market and their short holdings to appreciate less than the market. Similarly, in a declining market, they expect their short holdings to fall more rapidly than the market falls and their long holdings to fall less

Figure 2-8 Equity Hedge Strategy Performance
January 1990–December 2002

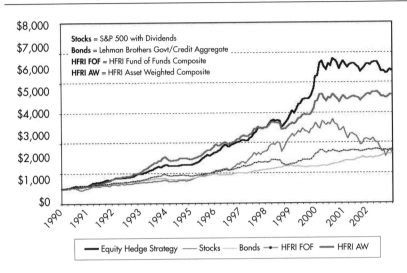

Stocks = S&P 500 with Dividends	
Bonds = Lehman Brothers Govt/Credit Aggregate	
HFRI FOF = HFRI Fund of Funds Composite	
HFRI AW = HFRI Asset Weighted Composite	

— Equity Hedge Strategy —— Stocks ····· Bonds ··•·· HFRI FOF ═══ HFRI AW

rapidly than the market. Profits are made when long positions appreciate and stocks sold short depreciate. Conversely, losses are incurred when long positions depreciate and/or the value of stocks sold short appreciates. The source of return of Equity Hedge is similar to that of traditional stock-picking trading strategies on the upside, but it uses short selling and hedging to attempt to outperform the market on the downside. Some Equity Hedge managers are "value" oriented, others are "growth" oriented, while a third category is "opportunistic" depending on market conditions.

EQUITY HEDGE SUBSTRATEGIES

In the growth subcategory, managers tend to have a long bias toward growth stocks. A significant positive correlation to growth indices such as the Russell 1000 Growth and the Nasdaq composite are to be expected. Short positions in value names may serve to further magnify the growth bet. Risk levels are determined by use of leverage, overall net exposure, net sector exposures, position concentration, and use of cash.

Managers in the value subcategory tend to have a long bias toward value stocks. A significant positive correlation to value indices such as the Russell 1000 Value or Barra Value may be observed. Short positions in growth names may serve to further magnify the value bet. Risk levels are determined by use of leverage, overall net exposure, net sector exposures, position concentration, and use of cash.

Managers in the opportunistic subcategory do not have a style bias or directional bias toward the market. Style and sector concentrations will be determined at the manager's discretion depending on current market opportunities. Returns are characterized by a variable, non-systemic, or low-correlation relationship to equity market indices. Risk levels are determined by use of leverage, overall net exposure, net sector exposures, position concentration, and use of cash.

EQUITY MARKET NEUTRAL

Equity Market Neutral strategies strive to generate consistent returns in both up and down markets by selecting equity positions with a total net portfolio exposure of zero. Managers hold a number of long equity positions and an equal, or close to equal, dollar amount of offsetting short positions for a total net exposure close to zero. A zero net exposure is referred to as *dollar neutrality* and is a common characteristic of all Equity Market Neutral managers. By taking long and short positions in equal amounts, the conservative Equity Market Neutral managers seek to neutralize the effect that a systemic change will have on values of the stock market as a whole. Most, but not all, Equity Market Neutral managers extend the concept of neutrality to risk factors or characteristics such as beta, industry, sector, investment style, and market capitalization. In all Equity Market Neutral portfolios, stocks expected to outperform the market are held long, and stocks expected to underperform the market are sold short. Returns are derived from the long/short spread, or the amount by which long positions outperform short positions.

Figure 2-9 Equity Market Neutral Strategy Performance
January 1990–December 2002

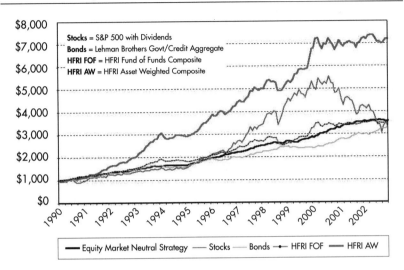

EQUITY MARKET NEUTRAL SUBSTRATEGIES

The fundamental substrategy involves managers who use fundamental research to select long and short portfolios. This is essentially an Equity Hedge strategy with the added constraint of dollar neutrality. Aggressive managers have mismatched long and short portfolios seeking to maximize return on both sides, and are more properly categorized for risk purposes as Opportunistic Equity Hedge. Conservative managers do their stock picking within a controlled risk framework, often ending up with beta and sector neutrality. Risk levels are determined by use of leverage, overall net exposure, net sector exposures, position concentration, and use of cash.

For the quantitative substrategy, managers use quantitative screens to rank stocks and build dollar, beta, and sector neutral portfolios. The process often leaves little room for human discretion. Managers are distinguished by the inputs into their multi-factor models. Conservative exposures usually are designed to yield a stream of returns equal to LIBOR plus a few percentage points.

Risk levels are determined by use of leverage, overall net exposure, net sector exposures, position concentration, and use of cash. Leverage is of particular importance in this category.

Statistical arbitrage managers use statistical models to identify sometimes very small statistical anomalies between equity securities while maintaining dollar neutrality. Statistical arbitrage strategies are characterized by very high turnover and an emphasis on the execution of trades. Many statistical arbitrage managers run multiple statistical models simultaneously to generate trade ideas.

EVENT DRIVEN

Event Driven investment strategies, or "corporate life cycle investing," are based on investments in opportunities created by significant transactional events, such as spin-offs, mergers and acquisitions, industry consolidations, liquidations, reorganizations, bankruptcies, recapitalizations, share buybacks, and other extraordinary corporate transactions. Event Driven trading involves attempting to predict the outcome of a particular transaction as well as the optimal time at which to commit capital to it. The uncertainty about the outcome of these events creates investment opportunities for managers who can correctly anticipate them. As such, Event Driven trading embraces Merger Arbitrage, Distressed Securities, value with a catalyst, and special situations investing.

Some Event Driven managers utilize a core strategy, while others opportunistically make investments across the range when different types of events occur. Dedicated Merger Arbitrage and Distressed Securities managers should be seen as stand-alone options, whereas Event Driven is a multi-strategy approach. Instruments include long and short common and preferred stocks, as well as debt securities, warrants, stubs, and options. Managers may also utilize derivatives such as index put options or put option spreads to leverage returns and "hedge out" interest rate and/or market risk. The success or failure of this type of strategy usually depends on whether the manager accurately predicts the outcome and timing of the transactional event.

Figure 2-10   Event Driven Strategy Performance
              January 1990–December 2002

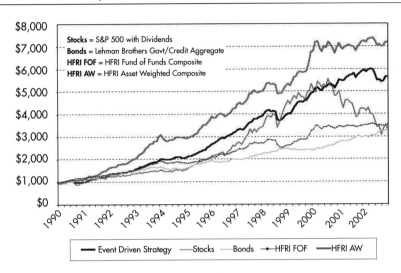

Event Driven managers do not rely on market direction for results; however, major market declines, which would cause transactions to be repriced or to break apart, and risk premiums to be reevaluated, may have a negative impact on the strategy.

EVENT DRIVEN SUBSTRATEGIES

Among the three substrategies within this category, value with a catalyst essentially is a long/short equity strategy utilizing event analysis to determine positions. Managers take positions by determining upside or downside potential of a stock if an event occurs or does not occur, and the probability that the event will occur. Risk levels are determined by use of leverage, overall net exposure, net sector exposures, position concentration, and use of cash.

In the special situations substrategy, managers often use distressed-type analysis to invest in companies that are not in bankruptcy, and that generally use more liquid securities than a pure distressed player. These positions may include orphan equities situations involving reorganizations or spin-offs. Risk levels are determined by use of leverage, overall net exposure, net sector exposures, position concentration, and use of cash.

The opportunistic substrategy involves managers who utilize multiple event strategies, including Merger Arbitrage, Distressed Securities, value with a catalyst, and special situations investing. Returns are determined by competency in each event strategy and asset allocation between strategies. Risk levels are determined by strategy concentrations, use of leverage, overall net exposure, net sector exposures, position concentration, and use of cash.

FIXED INCOME

Fixed Income strategies are "alternative" approaches to traditional, long-only fixed income investments, and include arbitrage and opportunistic strategies. Arbitrage strategies involve investing in one or more fixed income securities and hedging against underlying market risk by simultaneously investing in another fixed income security. Managers seek to capture profit opportunities presented by what are usually small pricing anomalies, while maintaining minimum exposure to interest rates and other systemic market risks. In most cases, managers take offsetting long and short positions in similar fixed income securities, which are mathematically or historically interrelated, when that relationship is temporarily distorted by market events, investor preferences, exogenous shocks to supply or demand, or structural features of the fixed income market. These positions could include corporate debt, U.S. Treasury securities, U.S. agency debt, sovereign debt, municipal debt, or the sovereign debt of emerging market countries. Trades often involve swaps and futures. Trading managers realize a profit when the skewed relationship between the securities returns to a normal range, or "converges."

Managers often try to neutralize interest rate changes and derive profit from their ability to identify similar securities that are mispriced relative to one another. Because the prices of fixed income instruments are based on yield curves, volatility curves, expected

Figure 2-11 Fixed Income Strategy Performance
January 1990–December 2002

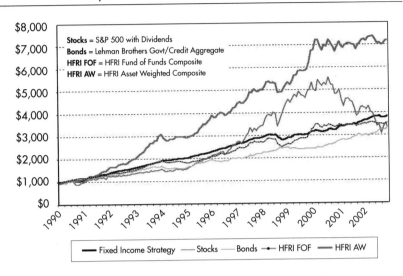

cash flows, credit ratings, and special bond and option features, they must use sophisticated analytical models to identify pricing disparities. The strategy often involves significant amounts of leverage. Opportunistic fixed income strategies may be long or short in a variety of fixed income instruments, essentially offering what a manager considers a "best of" the fixed income markets.

FIXED INCOME SUBSTRATEGIES

Of the two substrategies, arbitrage involves long and short trades of related fixed income securities in a fashion intended to neutralize market directional factors such as interest rates. Risk levels are determined by use of leverage, overall net exposure, net sector or security type exposures, position concentration, credit exposure, duration, and geographical exposure. Leverage is of particular importance in this category.

In the opportunistic subcategory, long and short fixed income instruments that are not necessarily related are traded. The strategy

Figure 2-12   Macro Strategy Performance
             January 1990–December 2002

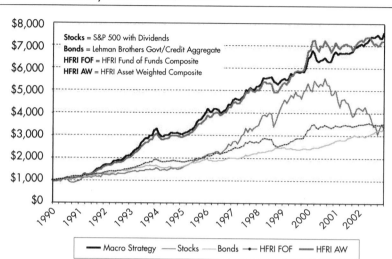

may be directional and involve relative evaluation of fixed income sectors. Risk levels are determined by use of leverage, overall net exposure, net sector or security type exposures, duration, credit exposure, position concentration, and geographical exposure.

MACRO

Macro strategies attempt to identify extreme price valuations in stock markets, fixed income markets, interest rates, currencies, and commodities and make bets on the anticipated price movements in these markets, sometimes in a leveraged fashion. Trades may be designed as an outright directional bet on an asset class or geographical region (e.g., long Japanese equities), or be designed to take advantage of geographical imbalances within an asset class (e.g., German 10-years relative to U.S. 10-years). To identify extreme price valuations, managers generally employ a top-down global approach that concentrates on forecasting how global macroeconomic and political events affect the valuations of financial instruments.

These approaches may be either systematic or discretionary.

The strategy has a broad investment mandate, with the ability to hold positions in practically any market with any instrument. In general, managers try to identify opportunities with a definable downside and favorable risk/reward characteristics. Profits are made by correctly anticipating price movements in global markets and having the flexibility to use any suitable investment approach to take advantage of extreme price valuations. Managers may use a focused approach or diversify across approaches. They often pursue a number of base strategies to augment their selective large directional bets.

MACRO SUBSTRATEGIES

The discretionary substrategy follows versions of the older Soros/Steinhardt/Robertson[3] models of making big directional and relative value bets based on discretionary decision making. Risk levels are determined by strategies employed, use of leverage, overall net exposure, net sector, country and asset class exposures, position concentration, and use of cash. Aggressive strategies tend to be more directional, while conservative strategies may involve some relative value analysis.

For systematic managers, buy and sell signals are generated automatically through quantitative and technical models. Risk levels are determined by strategies employed, use of leverage, overall net exposure, net sector, country and asset class exposures, position concentration, and use of cash. Aggressive strategies tend to be more directional, while conservative strategies may involve some relative value analysis.

MARKET TIMING

Market Timing involves allocating assets among investments by switching into investments that appear to be at the start of an uptrend and switching out of investments that appear to be starting a downtrend. This primarily consists of switching between mutual funds and money markets. Typically, technical trend-following

Figure 2-13 Market Timing Strategy Performance
January 1990–December 2002

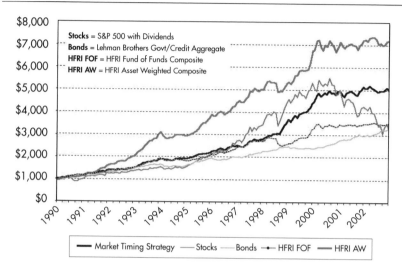

indicators are used to determine the direction of a fund and to identify buy and sell signals. In an up move "buy signal," money is transferred from a money market fund into a mutual fund in an attempt to capture a capital gain. In a down move "sell signal," the assets in the mutual fund are sold and moved back into the money market for safe keeping until the next up move. The goal is to avoid being invested in mutual funds during a market decline.

MERGER ARBITRAGE

Merger Arbitrage, also sometimes known as Risk Arbitrage, involves investing in securities of companies that are the subject of some form of extraordinary corporate transaction, including acquisition or merger proposals, exchange offers, cash tender offers, leveraged buyouts, proxy contests, recapitalizations, restructurings, or other corporate reorganizations. These transactions generally involve the exchange of securities for cash, other securities, or a combination of cash and other securities. Typically, a manager might purchase the

Figure 2-14   Merger Arbitrage Strategy Performance
January 1990–December 2002

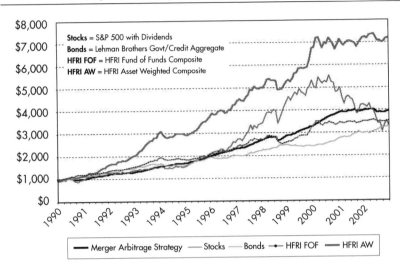

stock of a company being acquired or merging with another company and sell short the stock of the acquiring company. A manager engaged in merger arbitrage transactions derives profit (or loss) by realizing the price differential between the price of the securities purchased and the value ultimately realized from their disposition. The success of this strategy usually depends on the consummation of the proposed merger, tender offer, or exchange offer. Managers may use equity options as a low-risk alternative to the outright purchase or sale of common stock. In certain cases where the outcome of a merger is very doubtful, the manager may short the deal by reversing the positions and going short the target and long the acquiring firm.

MERGER ARBITRAGE SUBSTRATEGIES

In merger arbitrage there are a few factors that translate into differences in strategy returns, but very few managers consistently stay in one niche, so the only significant groupings are risk groups.

Risk levels are determined by position concentration, use of leverage, complexity of deals, use of cash, market cap of mergers, and geography.

RELATIVE VALUE ARBITRAGE

Relative Value Arbitrage is a multiple investment strategy approach. The overall emphasis is on making "spread trades," which derive returns from the relationship between two related securities rather than from the direction of the market. Generally, managers will take offsetting long and short positions in similar or related securities when their values, which are mathematically or historically interrelated, are temporarily distorted. Profits are derived when the skewed relationship between the securities returns to normal. In addition, Relative Value managers will decide which relative value strategies offer the best opportunities at any given time and weight each strategy accordingly in their overall portfolio. Relative Value strategies may include forms of fixed income arbitrage, including mortgage-backed arbitrage, merger arbitrage, convertible arbitrage, statistical arbitrage, pairs trading, options and warrants trading, capital structure arbitrage, index rebalancing arbitrage, and structured discount convertibles (which are more commonly known as Regulation D securities) arbitrage.

RELATIVE VALUE SUBSTRATEGIES

By definition this is a multiple strategy approach in which strategy weightings vary over time. While this does not lend itself to substrategy classification, managers can be evaluated by which strategies they include, or in some cases, by those that they exclude from their portfolios. Returns are determined by competency in each arbitrage strategy and asset allocation between strategies. Risk levels are determined by strategy concentrations, use of leverage, overall net exposure, net sector exposures, position concentration, and use of cash.

Figure 2-15 Relative Value Arbitrage Strategy Performance
January 1990–December 2002

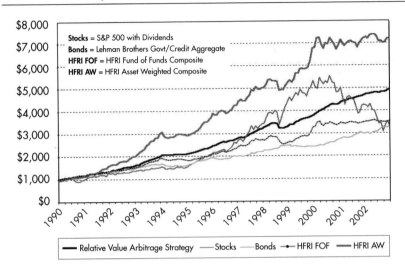

SECTOR LONG/SHORT

Sector strategies combine core long holdings of equities with short sales of stock or sector indices within a group of companies or segment of the economy that are similar either in what they produce or who their market is. Managers combine fundamental financial analysis with industry expertise to identify the best profit opportunities in the sector. Net exposure of sector portfolios may range anywhere from net long to net short depending on market and sector specific conditions. Managers generally increase net long exposure in bull markets for the sector and decrease net long exposure or may even be net short in bear markets for the sector. Generally, the short exposure is intended to generate an ongoing positive return in addition to acting as a hedge against a general sector decline. In a rising market for the sector, sector managers expect their long holdings to appreciate more than the sector and their short holdings to appreciate less than the sector. Similarly, in a declining market, they expect their short holdings to fall more rapidly than the sector falls and

Figure 2-16   Sector Strategy Performance
             January 1990–December 2002

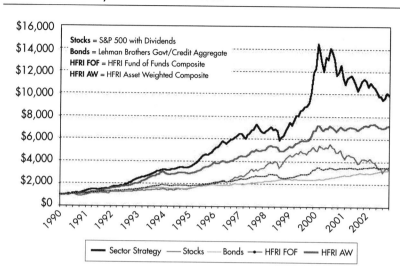

their long holdings to fall less rapidly than the sector. Profits are made when long positions appreciate and stocks sold short depreciate. Conversely, losses are incurred when long positions depreciate and/or the value of stocks sold short appreciates.

SECTOR LONG/SHORT SUBSTRATEGIES

Each meaningful sector represents a substrategy. Currently, the sectors with meaningful numbers of funds dedicated to them are: technology, health care/biotech, energy, financial, and real estate. Risk levels are determined by net exposure, position concentration, and use of leverage.

SHORT SELLING/SHORT BIAS

Short Selling strategies seek to profit from a decline in the value of stocks. The strategy involves selling a security the investor does not own in order to take advantage of a price decline the investor

Figure 2-17   Short Selling Strategy Performance
             January 1990–December 2002

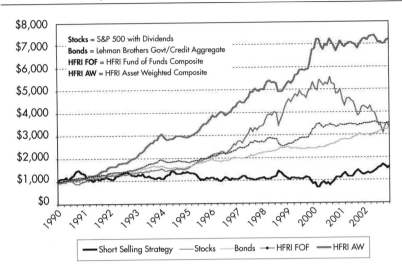

anticipates. Managers borrow the securities from a third party in order to deliver them to the purchaser. Managers eventually repurchase the securities on the open market in order to return them to the third party lender. If the manager can repurchase the stock at a lower price than for what it was sold, then a profit is made. In addition, managers earn interest on the cash proceeds from the short sale of stock. If the price of the stock rises, then the manager incurs a loss. This strategy is seldom used as a stand-alone investment. Because of its negative correlation to the stock market it tends to produce outsized returns in negative environments, and can serve as "disaster insurance" in a multimanager allocation. Some managers may take on some long exposure but remain net short, or short biased. Short Bias strategies are much less volatile than pure short selling exposure, but they do not provide as much upside in severely negative equity markets.

SUMMARY

Hedge fund investment approaches can be categorized into a variety of distinct strategies. For each strategy, there are multiple variations called substrategies. Most hedge fund managers are specialists pursuing a specific strategy and substrategy, although some use two or more strategies and multiple substrategies. In constructing their portfolio, fund of funds managers will select hedge funds based on strategies and substrategies they follow. The selection of a hedge fund is, in effect, a substrategy selection. Which strategies are selected and how they are weighted in a portfolio will depend on the performance goals of a fund of funds and the risk and return outlook that the fund of funds manager has for the strategies.

Chapter Notes

1. Hedge Fund Research, Inc. maintains and manages a database of hedge fund and fund of funds performance and is part of the HFR group of companies.

2. Joseph Nicholas, *Investing in Hedge Funds* (Bloomberg Press, 1999) and Joseph Nicholas, *Market-Neutral Investing* (Bloomberg Press, 2001).

3. In the late 1980s and early 1990s the largest hedge funds were macro funds run by Julian Robertson (Tiger Management), George Soros (Soros Fund Management), and Michael Steinhardt (Steinhardt Partners).

Fund of Funds Mechanics and the Two-Tiered Structure

3

IN CONSIDERING THE ORGANIZATION, operations, and features of a fund of funds, it is helpful to look at it within the framework of an investment fund that invests in other investment funds. This "two-tiered" structure, combined with the benefits the fund of funds seeks to offer over that of direct hedge fund investments, characterizes the purpose, functions, and activities of a fund of funds.

A fund of funds has many structural similarities to a hedge fund. Both rely on the same securities law exemption to avoid registration and regulation as an investment company in order to offer unregistered securities to investors. As is the case with single manager hedge funds, a fund of funds can be offered through onshore and offshore investment vehicles. Similarities also extend to terms such as liquidity, reporting, and redemption. Funds of funds features are dependent upon those of the underlying hedge funds in which they invest and, as a result, cannot offer superior treatment to that of the underlying hedge funds without assuming risk or cost, or both.

Because of the many similarities between the fund of funds and the underlying hedge funds, an action to be accomplished at the fund of funds level must be duplicated at the hedge fund level. Principal among these are

■ Investing
■ Redeeming
■ Reporting
■ Issuing performance reports/performance calculation
■ Completing audits and tax returns

For example, in order for a fund of funds to calculate its performance, it first must know the performance of all of its underlying hedge funds. Only then can the fund of funds' performance be determined. If even one hedge fund does not report, it is not possible to calculate the fund of funds' performance. Similarly, when an investor wishes to redeem an investment, the investor gives notice to the fund of funds. If the fund of funds has no investments coming in to offset the redemption, then it must determine from which underlying hedge fund or hedge funds it will, in turn, redeem. The fund of funds must then give its redemption notice in accordance with the requirements of each hedge fund, including the period of redemption (monthly or quarterly) and the required notice period. The notice period specifies the number of days in advance that the investor must notify the fund in order to receive the payment of cash or securities. If the notice period is missed, then the redemption occurs at the next redemption period. Another important specification is the number of days after the redemption date that the money will actually be paid out or settled. Compared to selling a stock or mutual fund, this process is difficult. Before the fund of funds can send funds to the investor, it must give notice to the underlying hedge fund manager or managers and wait for the hedge fund to comply with its redemption payment policies.

The ownership of a fund of funds' interest also brings with it a group of rights governing the mechanics of the relationship between the investor and the fund of funds. This includes subscription, redemption, investment management, and calculation of fees and expenses. This group of rights and "features" are not uniform and may vary from fund to fund.

STRUCTURAL CONSIDERATIONS

ORGANIZATION STRUCTURE

A fund of funds entity can be organized in a number of ways, including as a limited partnership (LP), a limited liability company (LLC), an offshore corporation, or a trust. Depending on the structure, the type of interest held by an investor will differ. For example, if the fund of funds is organized as a limited partnership, the investors are the limited partners. If organized as an LLC, they are members. However, the purpose and general characteristics of the fund remain the same. The main activities are also the same: to gather investor assets and to invest those monies.

The fund of funds manager charged with operating the fund of funds typically organizes the fund (whether as a partnership, corporation, or LLC) and is responsible for its administration, compliance, reporting, client service, accounting, and investment advising. In the case of a limited partnership, the general partner usually acts as fund manager. If the fund of funds is formed as an LLC, the management company acts as the managing member.

COMPANY STRUCTURE

An investor needs to understand the nature of the legal entity of the asset management company and how the ownership structure of the firm has evolved over time. Fund of funds investors should also look to understand what the responsibilities of the employees of the firm are. The legal structure could be a partnership, a corporation, or a limited liability company, but more importantly, the ownership structure can give indications of the leadership, direction, and influence that might affect the company, as well as indications as to where the business may be going in the future. Is it owned by the employees? Is it owned by a competitor? What kinds of changes have occurred over time? What has the company accomplished? Investors will need to evaluate the continuity of the management, how management is compensated, and how these factors may affect the fund of funds' performance in the future.

The company structure allows you to see how the company is organized along business disciplines and which people are responsible for each area of the business. Look for staffing, separation of disciplines (for example, investment management versus operations versus risk management), and depth of personnel.

Funds of funds are often described as "unregulated." This means that they are subject to only limited regulatory oversight by the Securities and Exchange Commission. The fund of funds manager may be registered with the SEC, or he may be exempt from registration. Similarly, the fund of funds can be either a registered investment company or an exempt entity. The trend is toward registration of funds of funds. Although regulatory and educational hurdles have limited the ability to deliver these products to the general public, it is expected that registered funds of funds will become increasingly accessible and acceptable methods of accessing hedge fund returns.

DOMICILE

Funds can be domiciled in a number of states within the United States (onshore funds) or somewhere outside the U.S. (offshore). Almost one-third of funds of funds are domiciled in Delaware, one-fifth are domiciled in the Cayman Islands, and another one-fifth are in the British Virgin Islands. (See *Figure 3-1*.)

As Figure 3-1 reveals, most offshore funds of funds are domiciled in either the British Virgin Islands or the Cayman Islands, both of which have become havens for offshore money for a variety of reasons, including tax benefits and their superior financial infrastructure.

Figure 3-1   Fund of Funds Domicile

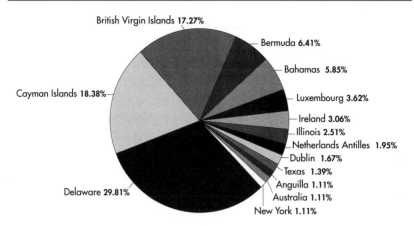

Other: One fund each in Connecticut, Guernsey, Isle of Man, Massachusetts, Minnesota, Nebraska, and North Carolina. Two funds each in Georgia and Washington. Three funds each in California and Curaco.

SUBSCRIPTIONS AND REGISTRATION EXEMPTIONS

Interests in onshore funds of funds are sold to investors by way of a subscription to a privately offered security subject to an exemption from registration. These exemptions restrict how the fund can be marketed and sold and also restrict the type and qualification of the investor. The two primary exemptions are explained in the Exclusion of Investment Company Act of 1940, sections 3(c)1, which limits the number of purchasers to one hundred "beneficial owners," and 3(c)7, which waives registration if no more than five hundred "super-qualified," high-net-worth investors are involved.

MINIMUM INVESTMENT SIZE

Hedge interests in funds of funds are sold to investors by way of subscription, and the money received from investors is pooled. These pooled funds, in turn, are allocated to underlying hedge funds that purchase securities according to the fund's specific investment strategy. The pooling of money is beneficial to investors since it allows investors to invest in multiple hedge funds without having to meet the individual managers' minimum investment requirements. Unlike many hedge funds, which have minimum initial investments of $1 million, the majority of funds of funds have minimum investment requirements of less than $1 million. (See *Figure 3-2*.)

Fifty-seven percent of the funds of funds in a survey of U.S.–based firms conducted in 2002 by the Alternative Investment Management Association (AIMA) have a minimum investment requirement of $250,000 or less, while 35 percent have requirements of $100,000 or less. Only 3.06 percent of funds of funds have a minimum investment requirement of more than $1 million. This can be attributed to the economies of scale investors achieve by pooling their funds together. Fund of funds managers know that part of what makes their product attractive is the relatively low minimum investments necessary to join the partnership coupled with the buying power the pooling of assets from all of the partners creates.

Figure 3-2 Fund of Funds Distribution by Minimum Investment Size

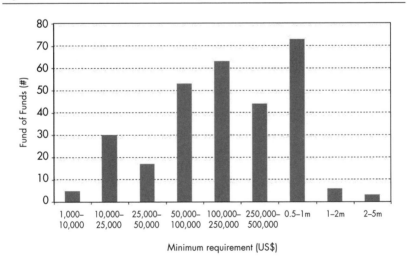

FEES

The value added by funds of funds comes at a cost: Investors must pay an extra layer of fees at the fund of funds level in addition to the fees paid to the underlying hedge fund managers. Most funds of funds charge an asset-based management fee, and many will also charge a performance-based incentive fee. Fund of funds fees vary considerably. The most common fee structure for funds of funds is a 1 percent management fee and 10 percent of net new profits. The second most common fee structure is 1.5 percent management fee with no incentive fee. According to the AIMA Survey conducted in 2002, the average management fee charged by funds of funds was 1.3 percent, and the maximum was 3 percent. For performance fees, the average was 9.9 percent, and the maximum 50 percent. In addition to charging a management fee and incentive fee, a fund of funds may also charge a selling commission and a redemption fee.

Management fees are usually charged as a percentage of assets, normally between 1 percent and 2 percent. Management fees are normally calculated and paid on a monthly or quarterly basis. For example, a fund of funds with $100 million in assets at the end of each quarter that charges a 1 percent management fee paid quarterly would earn $250,000 per quarter in management fees ($100,000,000 x 1% ÷ 4).

Some, but not all, funds of funds charge an incentive fee. An incentive fee, also called "carried interest," is charged as a percentage of net new profits. For example, an incentive fee of 10 percent means that 10 percent of the net new profits generated by the fund of funds is kept by the fund of funds. So, in this example, investors and the fund of funds split the profits 90/10, with the investor getting 90 percent of the profits. Incentive fees are usually calculated on a quarterly or annual basis.

Fund of funds incentive fees may be subject to two other features: a high-water mark and a hurdle rate. Almost all incentive fees are calculated using a high-water mark. The use of a high-water mark means that incentive fees are calculated only on new profits. This means that an investor does not pay for covering the same ground twice.

Consider a $100 million fund of funds that has a 10 percent incentive fee and no hurdle rate, earns $10 million in year one, loses $19 million in year two, and earns $10 million in year three. In year one, the fund of funds would charge a $1 million incentive fee. The fund (with no redemptions or additions) would have $109 million. In year two, the loss of $19 million brings the fund level to $90 million. In year three, the fund earns $10 million. Without a high-water mark, the fund of funds would earn a fee of $1 million— 10 percent of the profits for that year, even though the investor has not, over the three-year period, experienced any new profit. With a high-water mark, no incentive would be payable for year three, or in the future until the fund was above the high-water mark of $109 million.

A hurdle rate specifies a minimum level of return that the investor must receive before the incentive fee begins to be calculated. For example, a fund of funds with a 10 percent incentive fee and a 5 percent hurdle that earns 10 percent gross return would be calculated as follows: 100 percent of the first 5 percent return would go to the investor, as that would fall under the 5 percent hurdle rate. Of the next 5 percent, 4.5 percent would go to the investor and 0.5 percent would go to the fund of funds. Note that hurdle fees normally reset annually, so that if a fund of funds with a 5 percent hurdle is flat for a year, the hurdle is not aggregated with the following year's hurdle; in this way, the next year's hurdle rate is still 5 percent, not 10 percent. Of the forty-three funds of funds analyzed in the AIMA Survey, twenty-seven had no hurdle rates, five had hurdle rates of 10 percent, nine had a hurdle rate associated with the T-bill or LIBOR rates, and one fund had a hurdle rate of the S&P 500 return rate.

Another twist on the incentive fee concept is called a *claw-back*. Here the investor receives 100 percent of the profits within the hurdle and the fund of funds then receives the incentive fee percentage next; and any profits above are then split accordingly. For example, a fund of funds with a 10 percent hurdle and 10 percent incentive with a claw-back that grosses 20 percent would work as follows: The first 10 percent profits would go to the investor. The next 1 percent would go to the fund of funds as its 10 percent incentive claw-back. The remaining 9 percent would be split 90 percent to the investor and 10 percent to the fund of funds.

Funds of funds may also charge fees based on dollar size of investment, length of time/lockup, and fees upon investing (i.e., sales fees), and less commonly, redemption fees. Both sales fees and redemption fees are usually calculated as a percentage of assets. The fund of funds may also have a varying level of fees based on the size of the investment, with fee break points occurring above various levels.

Fund of funds expenses generally fall into two groups: organization and offering expenses, and ongoing expenses. Organization and offering expenses represent the up-front costs, such as accounting and legal expenses to set up the fund together with offering expenses incurred, such as printing and distribution of the offering memorandum and costs relating to marketing to the end investor. These fees are not always charged to the fund and may be absorbed by the fund management company. Ongoing expenses include accounting, administrative, legal, auditing, reporting, and other functions relating to the day-to-day administrative operation of the fund of funds.

Lockup, Redemption, and Liquidity

Liquidity for the fund of funds investor relates to the ability to take one's money out of the fund of funds. How liquid is the investment? A mutual fund has daily liquidity. A private equity fund may be locked up for three to five years. The term "redemption" is used to refer to the rights and process by which an investor gets its money back from its fund of funds investment. Hedge fund of funds' redemptions are normally available monthly or quarterly. In general, the underlying managers in a fund of funds determine the time frame for subscribing to or redeeming from the fund of funds. For instance, if each of the funds in a fund of funds allows for monthly subscriptions and quarterly redemptions, then the fund of funds will probably offer the same liquidity. However, if one of the funds invested in by the fund of funds allows only annual redemptions, the redemption process becomes more complicated. As *Figure 3-3* shows, most funds of funds allow for monthly subscriptions and quarterly redemptions.

An investor wishing to take some or all of its money out of a fund of funds will send a redemption notice. This formal request to the fund of funds for the return of money initiates a set process that determines on what date the value of the investor's assets to be returned will be established and when such monies will actually be sent to the investor.

The so-called notice period specifies the deadline date for receipt of the redemption notice in order to have the assets valued for the upcoming redemption period. Thus, a fund of funds with quarterly liquidity and a 45-day notice period must receive the redemption notice 45 days before the first day (or last day, as the case may be) of the next quarter in order to redeem for that date at that valuation. Investors must pay close attention to specifics such as business days versus calendar days. If the redemption notice is recorded after the 45-day deadline has passed, it will apply to the next quarter end—June 30 instead of March 31, for example.

Once the redemption date is established, the investor knows when his or her assets will be valued. However, when will the actual money be released and sent? It may be within a few days or as much as a month or more later. A portion of the assets may be held back until after the year-end audit. Why does it work this way? Because of the two-tier structure—the fact that a fund of funds is dependent on the characteristics of its underlying hedge funds. As mentioned before, a fund of funds must set its liquidity and redemption provisions to work with those of the underlying hedge funds it invests in. This coordination involves the period of redemption, the notice period of redemption, and the distribution of monies.

As evident in Figure 3-3, more than 75 percent of the funds of funds in the AIMA Survey allowed monthly subscriptions; less than 20 percent allowed quarterly subscription only, while the remainder have either daily (less than 1 percent), weekly, biweekly, or semiannual subscription policies.

Figure 3-3 Fund of Funds Distribution by Subscription and Redemption

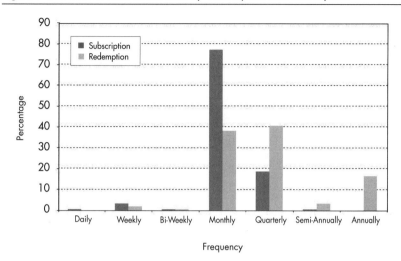

With respect to redemptions, although most funds have either monthly or quarterly redemption policies, more than 15 percent of the funds of funds in the survey permitted only annual redemptions. The nature of the hedge fund industry is one of precision and timing. Many strategies require that capital be allocated to a time-sensitive and highly contingent portfolio, sometimes utilizing thinly traded or illiquid securities. Furthermore, these strategies utilize highly sophisticated leveraging and hedging techniques that may require a long-term investment time horizon. Also because of these time and investment illiquidity sensitivities, the subscription and redemption process generally requires that the investor send notification within a predetermined, specified time period in order to place an order. Many funds of funds require at least a 15 business-day notification for either a subscription or a redemption.

Another concept relating to fund of funds liquidity is known as the *lockup period,* or simply *lockup.* The lockup refers to the period of time beginning with investment when redemptions are not allowed, or, in some cases, are allowed but are subject to a redemption fee. For example, a one-year lockup means that an investor may not redeem for a period of one year from the date of initial investment. After the lockup period has passed, the redemption period (e.g., occurring quarterly with a 45-day notice) will apply.

An investor's money may be subject to a significant lockup period lasting from three months to two years. Generally, the more illiquid the trading strategies pursued by the underlying hedge funds in the fund of funds, the longer the lockup period. According to data in the AIMA Survey of 2002, only 33 percent of funds of funds require an initial lockup; however, 70 percent of those require a lockup of six months or more.

Whereas the settlement date for traditional securities is normally three business days after the trade date, the settlement period for funds of funds can be as long as two weeks since there are a number of activities that must take place among the fund of funds, the underlying hedge funds within the fund of funds, and the specific investments within the hedge funds.

THE FUND OF FUNDS MANAGEMENT COMPANY

The fund of funds manager has two functions: One is to seek out investors, educate them on the investment benefits, accumulate the assets from investors, and report on and explain investment activities and performance; the second is to follow the hedge fund industry, determine strategy weightings, conduct due diligence, and select individual fund managers expected to outperform. The fund of funds manager allocates to and manages the investments, rebalancing, and redemptions in the underlying hedge funds. These functions are overseen by the fund of funds management company. Many management companies operate more than one fund of funds.

The asset accumulation functions begin with the design of the fund of funds. Normally, a fund of funds has identifiable objectives and goals; this is what is "sold" to the investor. It attempts to meet these goals through investment in the underlying hedge funds it chooses. In this effort, the second function of investing the fund of funds' assets into hedge funds is integrated with and guided by the first function. In essence, the fund of funds acts to match investment capital with hedge fund investment opportunities within stated investment strategy parameters.

MANAGER DUE DILIGENCE AND SELECTION

A key function of any fund of funds is selecting appropriate managers to achieve stated risk and return objectives. Performance differentials between managers pursuing similar strategies (as represented by the spread between upper and lower quartile managers) can be significant. These differences are largely attributable to the loose strategy definitions prevalent in the hedge fund industry, the lack of accepted benchmarks, and the ability of managers to use all the tools at their disposal to produce returns. As investments in hedge funds become more accepted, and hence, institutionalized, we would expect to see definitions become more specific. This should result in reduced dispersion between managers. That said, dispersion is likely to continue for the foreseeable future. Selecting which managers will be the top performers over any given period is a research-intensive process that requires in-depth due diligence, relationships, and a grasp of the underlying strategies, including the nuances that differentiate one subapproach from another.

Fund of funds managers need to maintain databases of information about hedge fund managers, including performance data, fund details, exposure information, firm histories, and biographies of key personnel. Information is gathered from the hedge funds themselves, data providers, prime brokers, industry contacts, hedge fund dedicated publications, and referrals from other industry sources. The databases are screened over various criteria to identify managers that warrant greater in-depth research. The manager selection process requires that fund of funds managers diligently watch the universe for new information. The fund of funds, then, can be thought of as a gatekeeper on behalf of its investors, efficiently sorting through the myriad of available managers to select the most promising. A detailed discussion of manager selection and due diligence is found in Chapter 9.

RISK MANAGEMENT

Fund of funds managers must also perform some level of risk management to ensure exposure objectives are met at the individual fund level as well as for the fund of funds. Risk management at the fund of funds level involves collecting risk data on underlying funds, aggregating risk exposures at the fund of funds level (including exposures to hedge fund strategies and other common risk factors), and creating performance attribution by fund and strategy. There is a qualitative element to risk management as well. A fund of funds manager should know what the worst-case scenario is for underlying hedge fund managers and be capable of avoiding scenarios with unacceptable risk. A more detailed discussion of fund of funds risk management practices is found in Chapter 10.

OPERATIONS

Operationally, a fund of funds must manage a range of relationships in order to coordinate the various internal departments and outside providers of administration, legal and compliance, accounting, and auditing services. Key outside service providers include a bank, an attorney, and an auditor. Furthermore, when and where necessary, outside service providers may also include a custodian, a trustee, and an accounting firm.

On their own, investors would be hard pressed to coordinate all of these activities. Efficient and cost-effective coordination by the investor would in fact be next to impossible. Yet because of the economies of scale generated by a fund of funds management company, which often operates multiple funds across which many of the fixed operational costs can be spread, it is actually relatively inexpensive for an individual to invest in a fund of funds.

The administration and operations staff of the fund of funds firm handles the processing of allocations and redemptions from managers, once they are selected, and the preparation and dissemination of performance information to the investors. Depending on the approach used by the fund of funds and the nature and size of its client base, these functions may represent a relatively small or large proportion of its operation.

PERFORMANCE AND EXPOSURE REPORTING

As has been noted, it is important that the structure of the fund of funds is in line with the reporting process and timing of the underlying hedge fund investments so as to provide for timely performance and portfolio reporting at the fund of funds level. For example, if a fund of funds tells investors it will report month-end performance results by the fifteenth of each month, then each underlying fund must report to the fund of funds sufficiently before the fifteenth of each month to allow time for the fund of funds to consolidate the data of each hedge fund into the summary fund of funds report.

In addition to performance reporting, a fund of funds will provide investors with varying levels of information about drivers of performance, the nature of underlying exposures, and hiring and firing of underlying hedge fund managers. Again, the level of information provided by the fund of funds is largely dependent on the level of information, or the level of transparency, provided by underlying hedge fund managers. Most funds of funds will tell investors that they have transparency, but the term is a slippery one, with definitions ranging from discussion transparency (i.e., the fund of funds discusses positioning with underlying managers) to full custodial position transparency (i.e., the fund of funds has custodial control of assets and hires a hedge fund manager as subadviser).

As noted earlier, the performance numbers reported by most funds of funds are estimates rather than hard numbers. The reason for this is that the performance of a fund of funds is dependent on the performance reported by the hedge funds in which it is invested. Because these reports from the hedge funds are usually recorded as estimates, the fund of funds performance must also be recorded as an estimate.

A related consideration is the fact that since the hedge funds are providing estimates, some must hold back assets until a fund year-end audit has been undertaken. Once the audit is completed and the actual performance is finalized, the held-back portion of the redemption can be paid. Since funds of funds invest in hedge funds with such provisions, they must be organized in a similar fashion or assume the risk of valuation change. The ability to pay cash to the investor at the fund of funds level is dependent on the return of such monies from the underlying hedge funds.

SUMMARY

Funds of funds are investment funds that invest in other investment funds—hedge funds. How they operate as businesses, the features they offer to investors, and the benefits they seek to offer investors over direct investment into hedge funds are determined by this two-tiered structure. Fund of funds aspects such as reporting and liquidity are limited by that offered by the underlying hedge funds. The low investment size, professional portfolio management, and investment diversification afforded by funds of funds are benefits superior to what a small or medium-sized investor could achieve on its own. The fund of funds' infrastructure and activities are based around providing these services.

Advantages and Disadvantages of Funds of Funds   4

ONCE A DECISION has been made to invest in hedge funds, the method of accessing the investment needs to be determined. A fund of funds can be a very effective way to invest in this area because hedge fund investing requires specialized knowledge and experience that is costly and time consuming when done properly—both in making initial manager selections and in conducting ongoing risk and investment management activities. When compared with the other approaches to investing in hedge funds, including selecting single manager funds for investment, creating a customized portfolio of hedge funds, or investing in a hedge fund index, funds of funds offer a number of benefits. The main advantages center on the following factors:

- Diversification
- Due diligence
- Risk management
- Manager selection
- Portfolio management
- Strategy selection
- Access to funds/capacity
- Consolidated reporting fees
- Performance

Funds of funds also have a number of drawbacks when compared to direct investments. The main disadvantages involve the following:

- Exposure to other investors' cash flows
- Fees
- Lack of control/customization
- Decreased transparency
- Performance[1]

ADVANTAGES

A number of important advantages to the fund of funds approach should be considered, as discussed below.

DIVERSIFICATION

A fund of funds by its nature provides diversification by investing its assets among a number of hedge funds. The diversification exists because of both the variety of investment strategies and the different substrategy approaches of managers within strategies. Because hedge funds often have high minimums, a fund of funds can provide smaller investors with a measure of diversification that they could not achieve directly. For an amount of capital significantly less than the required minimum necessary to invest in a group of hedge funds directly, an investor can diversify an investment among multiple hedge fund managers and strategies via a fund of funds. For example, an investor's $1 million investment into a fund of funds might provide exposure to twenty underlying hedge fund managers that individually would each require a $1 million minimum investment. This diversified exposure reduces the investment risk from any single hedge fund. By having a large number of funds, the impact of a total loss from one fund can be reduced to a few percentage points or less at the fund of funds level.

Of course, the amount of diversification can vary from fewer than five managers to more than fifty managers, with most funds of funds falling near the middle of this range. In evaluating fund of funds diversification benefits, consider the number of underlying funds invested in, the mix of strategies, the correlation between managers and strategies, and return and volatility objectives.

Funds of funds offer varied degrees of diversification, with some funds of funds highly diversified and others quite concentrated. An investor must sift through them to find the ones that offer the desired approach. By comparison, a custom portfolio can be designed to provide a specific level of diversification matched to the investor's requirements. Global index funds also offer broad diversification designed to match the diversification of the overall industry, while strategy index funds offer diversification within a specific strategy. Single hedge funds offer no diversification among strategies. Selecting a few single hedge funds over time may offer some limited diversification, though well below that of the other options.

DUE DILIGENCE

Funds of funds conduct professional due diligence on hedge fund managers they invest with as part of their basic organizational activities. The due diligence process consists of gathering all available information, verifying what can be verified, and evaluating the results. The process is both time and resource intensive. It is another significant benefit recognized by fund of funds investors.

Due diligence is conducted on hedge funds before they are selected as well as on an ongoing basis once an investment is made.

Significant resources, effort, and expertise are required to screen the thousands of funds and then to select the qualified few for inclusion in a fund of funds. Even if investors wished to allocate such resources, they would still be severely restricted by the time it would take to interview the number of candidates necessary to accomplish the due diligence process.

The amount of assets to be invested and the number of hedge funds in the portfolio are important factors when considering the cost-effectiveness of this option. Index funds can offer the same level of professional and cost-effective due diligence as a fund of funds. On the other hand, selecting an individual hedge fund can be expensive, as the cost of doing proper due diligence on a manager is high. Prior to selecting one manager, it may require the review of a number of managers. When these costs are spread over time and many investors in a fund, it can be greatly reduced compared to conducting it for a single investment. Due diligence for custom portfolios can be more expensive because direct costs may be incurred if the portfolio manager is not familiar with the hedge fund being investigated, or if the client wishes to conduct its own additional due diligence prior to investing.

Even with the increased press coverage of hedge funds and the various information sources providing hedge fund data, it is still an extensive and time-consuming process to evaluate, conduct due diligence, and maintain ongoing updates and reviews of their performance. By putting time and energy into identifying, screening, selecting, and monitoring managers, funds of funds provide a significant benefit.

RISK MANAGEMENT

In most cases, a fund of funds provides risk control over each fund it invests in, as well as the overall portfolio. Risk management is a benefit offered by funds of funds that investors rank highly; they are comforted by having an expert oversee the risk of their hedge fund investments. However, the actual amount of risk management varies widely among funds of funds. Also, it is important to make a broad distinction between "risk monitoring," activities to make one aware of the risk environment, and "risk management," or actions taken to reduce or eliminate a risk once it is identified. To conduct the highest level of risk management, the custody and control of fund of funds assets must be separated from the investment activities of the underlying hedge fund managers through the use of separately managed accounts. In this respect, index funds generally offer a higher level of risk management and oversight as the majority are constructed on separate account platforms.

For funds of funds that invest in hedge funds rather than separate accounts, risk management is limited to redeeming from one or more of the underlying funds. On the other hand, funds of funds that invest using separate accounts can address risk immediately and step in to make the direct portfolio adjustments. Where risk monitoring for some funds of funds might consist of a monthly conference call with each hedge fund manager to discuss performance and developments of the firm, others might conduct a daily independent pricing and trade reconciliation plus a daily risk exposure screening. Certainly, the ability to monitor and manage the risk of a fund of funds' underlying hedge fund investments has improved over time. This has been advanced by the increase in investor access to hedge fund position level and exposure information. Known as hedge fund "transparency," the topic has been an area of hot debate during recent years. (See Chapter 10 for a discussion of the varying levels of transparency.)

From the investor's perspective, it is important that the fund of funds has a program in place to identify risk issues and take such actions as are necessary to minimize their adverse impacts. In extreme cases, this means firing the hedge fund manager. In so-called closed-system transparent structures (i.e., investment structures where the custody, control, and pricing functions are separated from the trading functions), it might mean directing the hedge fund manager to reduce leverage or eliminate certain positions. In other cases, it may require reallocating assets to reduce overall fund of funds exposure to a specific risk. For example, a fund of funds' percentage allocation to specific markets might be part of its risk management strategy. If the maximum exposure to emerging markets is 10 percent, the fund of funds manager would reallocate money away from those underlying hedge fund managers with emerging market exposure in order to maintain the exposure at or below 10 percent of the overall fund of funds investment.

High-level risk monitoring and management are available for the other hedge fund investment options as well, provided the investor works with a professional adviser or fund of funds firm that provides such services, or builds its own infrastructure. To determine the cost effectiveness of such services, one should consider the risk management provided. In this area, more than in others, widely divergent levels of service exist for the same price. Where risk management is important, it pays to investigate and be selective.

PORTFOLIO MANAGEMENT: STRATEGY SELECTION AND MANAGER SELECTION

Funds of funds seek to generate excess return[2] above the industry return of the hedge fund strategies. For diversified funds of funds, this relates to the hedge fund industry as a whole—the collective asset-weighted performance of the set of hedge fund strategies. For more specified funds of funds, the expected return and exposure constraints may be in relation to a subset of hedge fund strategies. There is a broad choice of fund of funds options available to investors, which can be grouped into four categories, discussed in Chapter 5.

Each fund of funds offers a different "blend" of hedge fund strategies and managers. Fund of funds managers who can generate consistent excess performance over their peers offer a major benefit to investors. Funds of funds seek to generate this alpha in two ways: strategy selection and manager selection (which is actually substrategy selection).

A fund of funds will select or overweight certain hedge fund strategies that they expect will outperform and avoid or underweight other strategies that they expect will underperform. The composition of the fund of funds will differ from that of the overall hedge fund industry and therefore generate a distinct return. By overweighting and underweighting the various hedge fund strategies, a fund of funds manager attempts to deliver returns superior to the overall industry by moving into favored strategies and out of underperformers.

In addition to seeking outperforming strategies, funds of funds managers seek to select outperforming managers within each strategy. By choosing one manager within a strategy while excluding others, a fund of funds seeks to generate alpha or excess return over the market return of the strategy. Managers who consistently outperform peers tend to have either (1) an identifiable edge, be it talented personnel, experience, resources, an informational advantage, or (2) a unique approach that results in different and more profitable exposures than peers.

Because of the diversity of hedge fund investment approaches even within a single strategy, the selection of one hedge fund over another is often a substrategy choice, such as selecting a merger arbitrage fund that specializes in smaller-cap deals over one that invests only in large-cap deals. In this case, the manager choice is really a substrategy choice with its performance dependent more on the performance of the small-cap deals versus overall merger deals than on manager ability.

Similarly, custom portfolios seek to achieve excess returns through strategy selection and manager selection. Single hedge fund selection does as well. Index funds, however, differ. They seek to select a group of funds within each strategy that will track the performance of the market—in effect, deliver to investors the "beta" of the strategy. To do so, index funds need to include representative substrategies in manager selections rather than pick the expected outperformer. At the combined level, index funds seek to weight strategies in the same way they are represented in the market. Simply stated, index funds seek to match the hedge fund industry performance while funds of funds seek to outperform it. As in all investment endeavors, it is difficult to outperform the market after fees, and the same holds true with funds of funds. While some funds of funds persist in outperforming the hedge fund industry, the vast majority do not.

ACCESS TO FUNDS/CAPACITY

Another benefit of funds of funds for investors is access to hedge funds. This can fall into three categories: Access to hedge funds in general, access to hedge funds that investors could not otherwise invest in due to capital limitation, and access to hedge funds that are closed to new investment.

Almost all hedge funds are private investment funds and as such do not make their information publicly available. For an investor new to hedge funds, it is therefore difficult to be aware enough of what is available to get started. Databases and directories are commercially available and contain information about hedge funds that is privately collected. However, even with hedge fund databases as a starting point, there is still a significant amount of effort required to address the industry competently. Fund of funds managers, however, are in touch with the hedge fund universe on a regular basis, and they stay on top of the manager and strategy trends, developments, and performance. For many investors, this general level of access is a significant benefit.

The second level of access is based on an investor's capital limitations. Because of the high minimum investment required by hedge funds, an investor is limited in how many hedge funds it can invest in for a given amount of capital. For example, if an investor would like to diversify an investment among at least ten hedge funds, it would not be able to do so unless it had sufficient capital to meet each hedge fund's minimum investment requirement of $1 million. By combining that investor's $500,000 with the investments of a number of other investors, a fund of funds can access all ten hedge funds. This access through pooled buying power is a significant benefit of funds of funds.

The third level of access is the ability to invest with managers who have closed their funds to new investment. Some hedge fund managers close from time to time, refusing to take in any more investment assets at all, or to accept additional investments only from existing relationships. In the case of these funds, investors cannot invest even if they are aware of the hedge fund and have the minimum assets to invest with them. In such situations, funds of funds that can gain access from these "closed" managers, based on a pre-existing investment or relationship, are viewed as providing a significant benefit to investors.

Originally, funds of funds were a point of access to hedge funds for the novice accredited investor and the small investor. Lack of transparency, in all of its forms, proved to be a significant barrier to many who could invest in and benefit from a hedge fund. Very often, investors who wanted to invest in hedge funds needed to work with someone who knew and had a close, often personal relationship, with a hedge fund manager. As the industry expanded, the concept of access evolved. Some funds of funds attract investors with the claim that they have special access to managers or funds no longer open for new investments.

The access benefits of other investment options will depend on the relationship of the people and firms involved. Generally, existing products will have an edge over the new investments of a custom portfolio or single hedge fund investment.

CONSOLIDATED REPORTING

Funds of funds collect and consolidate performance data from all underlying funds each month. This information is then consolidated for the fund of funds' performance statement for the month just ended. As most hedge funds report performance estimates subject to a year-end audit, with few exceptions fund of funds performance reports are estimates as well. However, the industry is increasingly moving toward publishing firm monthly performance information.

As hedge funds are private, there is no uniform method or timing of reporting. Also, most funds of funds provide an explanation of performance that requires input from each underlying hedge fund manager. A fund of funds with investments in twenty to fifty underlying hedge funds must devote a significant amount of time and resources each month to review the materials provided and conduct meetings and conference calls with each manager to discuss performance issues.

Each year, funds of funds also prepare an audit as well as final performance and tax reportings. Again, coordinating a large number of underlying hedge funds requires huge expenditures of time and resources. This primarily administrative service provided by a fund of funds is highly valued by investors. Index funds offer the same benefits. Custom portfolios can offer similar treatments, although the expenses are not shared with other investors and therefore can be less cost-effective.

FEES

There are additional fees and expenses charged by a fund of funds above the costs of the underlying hedge funds. However, they can be seen as a fund of funds benefit when compared with the cost of doing the same job independently, because the costs of investing in multiple hedge funds is spread among many investors. Such arrangements provide the greatest savings to the smallest investor and diminishing cost-effectiveness as the amount of investment increases. For that reason, fees are listed as both an advantage for some and as a disadvantage for others. Custom portfolio services usually charge fund of funds fees, although they may be higher or lower depending on the level of services provided and the amount of the investment. Generally, larger investors who build custom portfolios can achieve fee breaks based on allocation size. Index funds may offer lower fees and present a lower-cost way to access the hedge fund industry or individual strategy returns.

PERFORMANCE

Funds of funds seek to generate outperformance relative to the hedge fund industry. This is done at the risk of underperformance. An important benefit is a fund of funds' ability to generate alpha above a passive index allocation. Similarly, custom portfolios seek to generate excess returns. By contrast, index funds aim to deliver the market return achieved by hedge fund investors generally. Historically, the vast majority have failed to outperform the hedge fund market after fees. Index funds are relatively new, but if they can deliver market returns and fund of funds performance trends persist, then index funds will represent a viable performance option for investors.

DISADVANTAGES

The disadvantages of fund of funds investing must also be taken into consideration and weighed against their benefits. They relate directly to the commingled nature of funds of funds and the fund layer between the investor and the hedge funds. The following discussion reviews the four main disadvantages.

EXPOSURE TO OTHER INVESTORS' CASH FLOWS

In most cases, a fund of funds commingles the assets of a number of investors. This collective pool of money is then invested in hedge funds. The disadvantage is that as the fund of funds handles investor inflows and outflows, it may not always be allocating in the most advantageous manner. Holding cash deleverages returns. Borrowing to redeem leverages the fund of funds. Such action may distort performance positively or negatively.

Index funds may also be subject to the impact of inflows and outflows, but they are designed to maintain industry exposure weightings at all times. Custom portfolios, with a single investor, are not exposed to this type of event.

FEES

Funds of funds charge another layer of fees and expenses in addition to those charged by the underlying hedge funds. A number of investors see this as a disadvantage. Of course, the services and infrastructure have a cost, and as discussed, value. Thus, the issues tend to center on the reasonable level of fees to be charged for the benefits delivered. As discussed previously in Chapter 3, according to the Alternative Investment Management Association (AIMA) survey conducted in 2002, the average fund of funds charges a management fee of 1.3 percent. The maximum management fee charged is 3 percent. For performance fees, the average is 9.9 percent, and the maximum is 50 percent. Given these costs, for larger investors or ones with greater expertise and infrastructure, it may be more cost-effective to select managers and manage the administration process as a custom portfolio. As most fund of funds benefits are also available in index funds, the extra fees are justified if the fund of funds can generate excess returns above the index after fees.

LACK OF CONTROL/CUSTOMIZATION

Because a fund of funds is a "one size fits all" proposition when managed as a commingled fund by a third party, the fund of funds form of investment, by definition, results in the investor giving up control over how the assets are invested and the fund management decisions are made. However, many investors prefer an investment program tailored specifically for their needs as well as allowing the investor to make decisions on how the fund of funds is managed. Therefore, the lack of control by the investor is seen by some to be a disadvantage to investing in a fund of funds, although some investors seek to counter this by investing in multiple funds of funds.

If an investor has enough capital, the investor can pursue direct investments into hedge funds or work with a fund of funds manager to create either a customized portfolio of hedge funds or a private fund of funds wherein the investor can design the allocation to fit the investor's specific objectives and parameters and thereby have discretion over the investment activities. Like funds of funds, index funds do not offer flexibility, although combining and weighting strategy index funds provides a degree of customization.

DECREASED TRANSPARENCY

By investing through a fund of funds, the investor does not have a direct relationship with the hedge funds in which it invests. Whatever level of transparency each hedge fund provides to investors is given to the fund of funds. Information gathered each day or month is evaluated by the fund of funds alone. In most cases, decisions are made based on this information without the investor's knowledge or input. Information is filtered through the fund of funds, resulting in a more opaque investment than direct investment with a hedge fund. In this respect, custom portfolios or single hedge funds can offer investors a high level of transparency. However, some funds of funds and index funds offer investors a high level of daily exposure and performance information.

SUMMARY

As a way of investing in hedge funds, a fund of funds is beneficial to both small and large investors. Smaller investors are given more access and more diversification through a fund of funds. Larger investors see that there is a cost savings in terms of time, energy, and resources devoted to selecting hedge funds and managing a portfolio. The administrative and due diligence services provided by funds of funds are extremely attractive, particularly when the investor does not possess the knowledge, expertise, and resources required to meet the challenge of fund of funds management. The fund of funds approach helps to simplify the decision process of the investor. On a micro level, the investor need only research fund of funds managers to discover those best suited to his or her objectives. On the macro level, the investor simply weighs the advantages and disadvantages and the benefits and drawbacks. Funds of funds are ideal for meeting a variety of investor needs. Investors should consider the pros and cons of fund of funds investing and whether the benefits outweigh the drawbacks.

Chapter Notes

1. Performance can be either an advantage or a disadvantage depending on the investor. Over time, funds of funds as a group have underperformed measures of hedge fund industry performance. This underperformance is at least in part due to the extra layer of fees associated with a fund of funds. The question for the investor is whether this cost is outweighed by the various benefits associated with a fund of funds investment.

2. Excess return and alpha are used interchangeably in this chapter to describe the excess return above a peer or strategy group of managers engaged in similar investment activities. Similarly, beta is used to describe the return associated with the strategy pursued, independent of manager skill. It is acknowledged that these usages may be inconsistent with the more precise mathematical definitions associated with the Capital Market Pricing Model.

PART 2

Historical Performance of Funds of Funds

Performance of Funds of Funds 5

M UCH OF THE POPULARITY and growth of funds of funds (FOFs) during the past ten years is due to the attractive returns they have produced. Funds of funds have performed well on both a risk-adjusted basis and when compared to the nominal performance of both the stock and bond markets. Since 1990,

Figure 5-1   Annualized Returns, 1990–2002

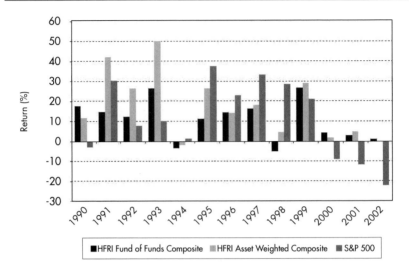

▪HFRI Fund of Funds Composite ▪HFRI Asset Weighted Composite ▪ S&P 500

funds of funds have delivered returns superior to that of the equity markets—not just in absolute returns, but with more consistency and less risk. The funds of funds performance was significantly less volatile than that of the equity markets. While they did not make as much in the highest-performing months, they also did not decline nearly as much during loss periods. Funds of funds are able to out-perform equities through compounding; they preserve capital and therefore have more money available to generate returns during profitable periods. As we shall see in this chapter, since 1990 funds of funds have generated consistent positive performance, preserved capital, and compounded profits.

Funds of funds have been less adroit at generating excess returns compared to the hedge fund industry in general. Some funds of funds outperform hedge fund industry returns, others do not; but on balance funds of funds have underperformed industry indices. Because funds of funds are such a large component of the hedge fund industry, they, in effect, are the industry, and so it approaches a "zero-sum" game for funds of funds to outperform the industry as a group. And, this is before funds of funds' fees and expenses.

Figure 5-2 Annualized Volatility, 1990–2002

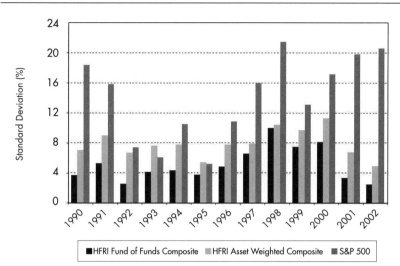

When comparing net performance, funds of funds underperform as a group, by approximately the amount of fees and expenses charged. It has also been argued that funds of funds have a more static portfolio management allocation approach that lags the shift in hedge fund strategy performance leadership.

So, in spite of attractive returns relative to traditional asset classes, an investor should consider a number of other factors related to funds of funds investing. For example, funds of funds generally charge management and performance fees on top of the underlying funds' fees. While the benefits of investing with a fund of funds, as reviewed in Chapter 4, generally merit the higher fees, one should consider whether a particular fund of funds adds enough value to justify the expense. Another example would be consistency of performance. Many funds of funds become popular after outperforming hedge fund industry indices for a period of time. Many of them then fail to outperform in the following periods. (See *Figures 5-1* and *5-2* for an illustration of this pattern in performance and volatility.)

This chapter reviews funds of funds' performance characteristics, such as returns, volatility, risk-adjusted returns, capital preservation, bull and bear market performance, average positive and negative returns, return distribution, correlation, and performance during stress periods. For purposes of analysis, we will use the HFRI Fund of Funds Index, which encompasses a universe of more than 400 funds of funds. This index calculates the average performance of funds of funds each month, net of fees and expenses. Since it consists of a large number of funds of funds, it is useful as a general indication of their performance. For comparative purposes, we employ standard stock and bond market benchmarks: the S&P 500, the MSCI World Index, and the Lehman Brothers Government/Credit Bond Index, as well as the HFRI Asset Weighted Composite Index representing hedge fund performance. We will also examine two time periods: January 1990 to December 2002, and January 2000 to December 2002. The longer-term analysis provides a good indication of fund of funds' performance over a full market cycle. The shorter time frame provides useful insight into fund of funds' returns during the most volatile period of stock market decline in the data set. This latter period is of particular interest since the long/short nature of hedge funds has been billed as a good investment to weather market downturns.

FUND OF FUNDS SUBSTRATEGIES

Funds of funds can be classified into various substrategies. We will introduce four core substrategies—Conservative, Strategic, Diversified, and Market Defensive—to augment the more general analysis and highlight differences among funds of funds. The general methodology used to categorize the funds of funds is based on risk and return characteristics, exposures to the various underlying hedge fund investment strategies, and sensitivities to systemic market factors. Outlined below are the four fund of funds subgroupings.

HFRI FUND OF FUNDS CONSERVATIVE INDEX

A fund of funds that is classified as Conservative may exhibit one or more of the following characteristics:

- The fund of funds seeks consistent returns by primarily investing in funds that engage in more "conservative" strategies such as Equity Market Neutral, Fixed Income strategies (primarily Arbitrage), Merger Arbitrage, Relative Value Arbitrage, and Convertible Arbitrage.
- The fund of funds exhibits a lower historical annual standard deviation than the HFRI Fund of Funds Index.
- The fund of funds performs consistently, regardless of market conditions.

HFRI FUND OF FUNDS STRATEGIC INDEX

A fund of funds that is classified as Strategic may exhibit one or more of the following characteristics:

- The fund of funds seeks outsized returns by primarily investing in funds that engage in more volatile, opportunistic strategies, often with significant weightings to Emerging Markets, Sector Long/Short, and Equity Hedge.
- The fund of funds exhibits a greater dispersion of returns and higher volatility compared to the HFRI Fund of Funds Index.
- The fund of funds outperforms the HFRI Fund of Funds Index in up equity markets and underperforms the index in down equity markets.

HFRI FUND OF FUNDS DIVERSIFIED INDEX

A fund of funds that is classified as Diversified may exhibit one or more of the following characteristics:

- The fund of funds is highly diversified and invests in a variety of strategies and among multiple managers.
- The fund of funds has a historical annual return and/or a standard deviation similar to the HFRI Fund of Funds Index.
- The fund of funds performance correlates closely to the HFRI Fund of Funds Index.

- The fund of funds shows performance and return distribution similar to the HFRI Fund of Funds Index.
- The fund of funds preserves capital and/or makes money in down equity markets and posts positive returns in up equity markets.

HFRI FUND OF FUNDS MARKET DEFENSIVE INDEX

A fund of funds that is classified as Market Defensive may exhibit one or more of the following characteristics:

- The fund of funds invests significant assets in funds that engage in strategies with negative correlations to equity markets such as short selling and managed futures.
- The fund of funds has a negative correlation to equity market indices.
- The fund of funds exhibits higher relative returns during down equity markets than during up equity markets.

Figure 5-3 FOF Returns, January 1990–December 2002

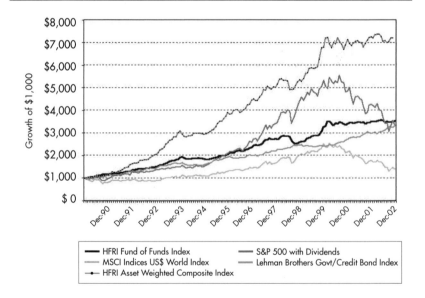

Figure 5-4 FOF Returns, January 1990–December 2002

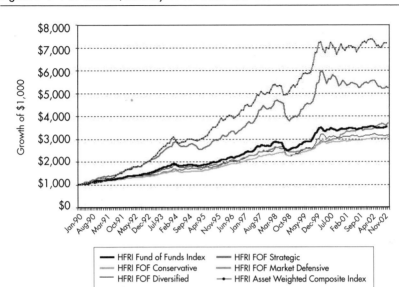

FUND OF FUNDS RETURNS 1990–2002

Funds of funds have demonstrated the ability to perform in diverse market conditions. They delivered strong returns during years when equity market performance was positive and when it was negative. Funds of funds produced annualized returns of more than 10.19 percent from January 1990 through December 2002. By comparison, the S&P 500 returned 9.65 percent, the MSCI 2.60 percent, the Lehman Govt/Credit Bond Index 9.70 percent, and the HFRI Asset Weighted 16.39 percent. On a return basis, the HFRI Fund of Funds Index outperformed all equity and bond indices over this period but fell considerably short of the HFRI Asset Weighted Composite. (See *Figure 5-3*.)

As illustrated in *Figure 5-4*, all fund of funds substrategies displayed strong performance during the period from January 1990 to December 2002. The HFRI Fund of Funds: Strategic Index generated an annualized return of 13.60 percent, the highest compared to the other strategies over the given period. This can be attributed to

Figure 5-5 FOF Returns, January 2000–December 2002

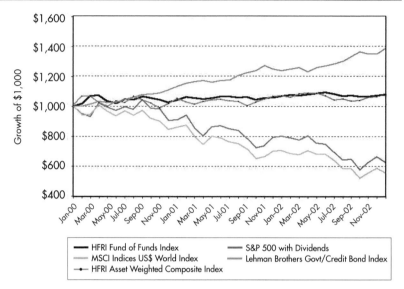

the more aggressive and opportunistic investment style of Strategic funds of funds. For example, many Strategic funds of funds concentrated their investments in Equity Hedge and Equity Non-Hedge Managers during the bull market period from November 1998 to February 2000. HFRI Fund of Funds: Conservative Index produced the lowest returns at 9.03 percent. This can be attributed to the priority of Conservative funds of funds to invest in strategies that display low volatility. The HFRI Fund of Funds: Diversified produced returns of 9.33 percent and the HFRI Fund of Funds: Market Defensive 10.56 percent.

FUND OF FUNDS RETURNS 2000–2002

In the period beginning from 2000, the difference in returns between funds of funds and equity indices was even more pronounced. From January 2000 to December 2002, funds of funds produced annualized returns of 2.62 percent versus –14.62 percent for the S&P 500, –16.39 percent for MSCI World, and 2.08 percent for HFRI

Figure 5-6 FOF Returns, January 2000–December 2002

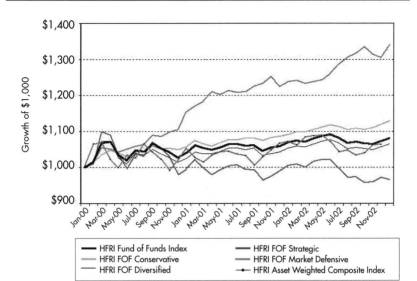

Asset Weighted Index. Bonds fared much better during this period, returning 11.57 percent. These results illustrate the ability of funds of funds to preserve capital during down markets. (See *Figure 5-5*.)

Among the fund of funds substrategies, the HFRI Fund of Funds: Market Defensive Index produced a 10.24 percent annualized return during the more recent time period, the highest among the fund of funds strategies. Market Defensive funds of funds were able to achieve superior returns because of their objective to invest in strategies that have negative correlation to equity indices such as Short Selling and Managed Futures. During this time period these strategies produced the highest returns of all the underlying hedge fund strategies. By contrast, the HFRI Fund of Funds: Strategic Index, which has the most sensitivity to the equity markets, produced a -1.16 percent return. Still, the performance significantly exceeded that of the market. The HFRI Fund of Funds: Diversified had a 2.12 percent return and the HFRI Fund of Funds: Conservative a 4.15 percent return. (See *Figure 5-6*.)

Figure 5-7 Rolling One-Year Volatility, January 1991–December 2002

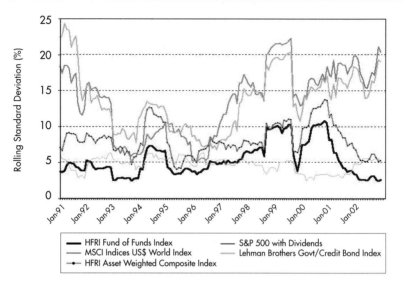

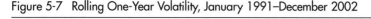

FUND OF FUNDS VOLATILITY 1990–2002

Volatility is one measure of the risk that funds of funds take to achieve their returns. *Figure 5-7* depicts rolling one-year volatility from 1991 to 2002 for funds of funds and the market indices. The relatively high risk of the equity indices is evident, with annualized volatility over the entire time period for the S&P 500 at 15.26 percent, and for the MSCI at 15.07 percent. Bond volatility was significantly lower at 4.96 percent. The HFRI Asset Weighted Index had 8.67 percent annualized volatility. Fund of funds volatility during this period was 5.94 percent, less than that of equities and just 18 percent more than bonds. Since 1990, the HFRI Fund of Funds Composite Indices have been less volatile and have experienced less downside deviation than either the S&P 500 or the MSCI World Index.

As shown in *Figure 5-8*, all fund of funds substrategies exhibit a significantly lower correlation than the equity indices. The HFRI Fund of Funds: Conservative Index produced the lowest annual-

Figure 5-8 Rolling One-Year Volatility, January 1991–December 2002

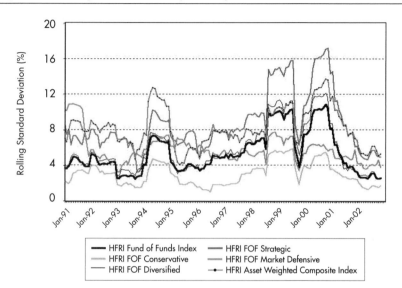

ized volatility for the entire period at 3.40 percent. This can be attributed to the Conservative fund of funds' concentration in low volatility arbitrage strategies. The HFRI Fund of Funds: Strategic Index, which among the fund of funds substrategies has the highest correlation to the equity indices, had the highest volatility at 9.63 percent. The volatility for HFRI Fund of Funds: Diversified was 6.39 percent and HFRI Fund of Funds: Market Defensive was 6.12 percent.

FUND OF FUNDS VOLATILITY 2000–2002

During the three-year period through 2002, stock market volatility increased to 18.75 percent on an annualized basis for the S&P 500 and 16.96 percent for MSCI World, with bond volatility at 4.39 percent. The HFRI Fund of Funds Index and the HFRI Asset Weighted Composite actually decreased slightly to 5.12 percent and 7.88 percent, respectively. Furthermore, as is shown in *Figure 5-9*, the volatility of the HFRI Fund of Funds Index decreased within

Figure 5-9 Rolling One-Year Volatility, January 2000–December 2002

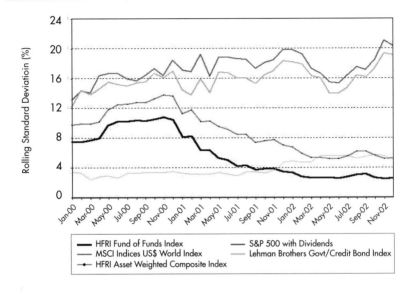

the period as the volatility of the equity indices was increasing. This can be attributed to shifts in strategy weightings at the fund of funds level as well as more conservative positioning by underlying hedge fund managers (as evidenced by a similar trend in the volatility of the HFRI Asset Weighted Index).

All fund of funds substrategies also showed slightly decreased volatility over the three-year period, as illustrated in *Figure 5-10*. The HFRI Fund of Funds: Conservative Index had the lowest volatility for the entire period at 2.62 percent. The HFRI Fund of Funds: Strategic Index had the highest volatility at 9.12 percent. The HFRI Fund of Funds: Diversified Index volatility was 5.40 percent, and the HFRI Fund of Funds: Market Defensive was 4.80 percent. Over time the various substrategy indices converged to a certain extent, reflecting less divergence in strategy exposures as well as more conservative positioning at the level of the underlying hedge fund managers.

Figure 5-10   Rolling One-Year Volatility, January 2000–December 2002

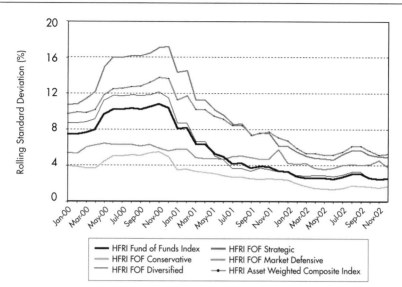

FUND OF FUNDS RETURN VERSUS VOLATILITY 1990–2002

By plotting risk (volatility) and return on one chart, we get a picture of the risk taken for the return achieved. *Figures 5-11* and *5-12* graphically present the classic relationship between risk (volatility) and reward (return) for the various indices.

It is immediately apparent that funds of funds have provided investors with returns superior to equities with bond-like volatility since 1990. Note that funds of funds have delivered significantly higher returns than the MSCI World Index, with lower risk. This can be explained in part by the geographical concentration of hedge funds, which have historically favored investment in U.S. companies and markets. Also note that the highest return is achieved by the HFRI Asset Weighted Composite, and while its risk is also higher, the risk/return ratio is very similar to those of the HFRI Fund of Funds and Lehman Bond indices. The relationships are even more

Figure 5-11   Return Versus Volatility, January 1990–December 2002

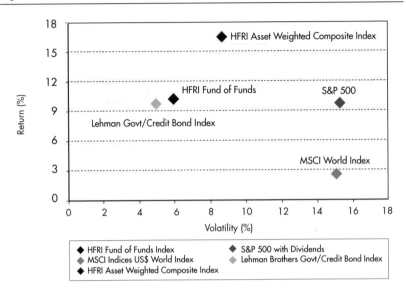

Figure 5-12   Return Versus Volatility, January 2000–December 2002

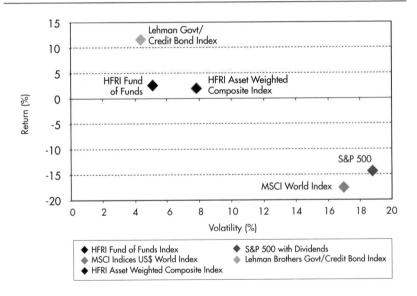

pronounced in the more recent period, during which the HFRI Fund of Funds Index reduced volatility while producing a positive return, whereas the equity indices produced negative returns with a greater level of volatility.

In plotting risk and return for the HFRI Fund of Funds Sub-strategy Indices, as illustrated in *Figures 5-13* and *5-14*, we can see that the substrategies fall on a risk spectrum with the HFRI Fund of Funds: Conservative Index providing the lowest risk and lowest return and the HFRI Fund of Funds: Strategic Index, the highest risk and highest return. Since the majority of the funds of funds are structured as multimanager, multistrategy, it is not surprising that the HFRI Fund of Funds: Diversified Index exhibits similar risk and return characteristics to the HFRI Fund of Funds Index. The risk spectrum also exists in the more recent period, but the return statistics change. Not surprisingly, the HFRI Fund of Funds: Market Defensive Index was the top performer followed by the HFRI Fund of Funds: Conservative Index. Both substrategies emphasize

Figure 5-13   Return Versus Volatility, January 1990–December 2002

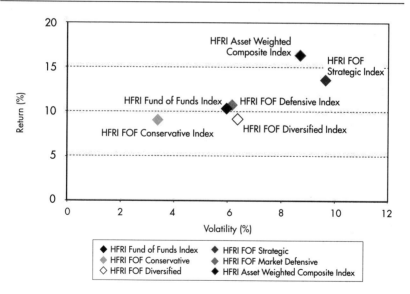

Figure 5-14 Return Versus Volatility, January 2000–December 2002

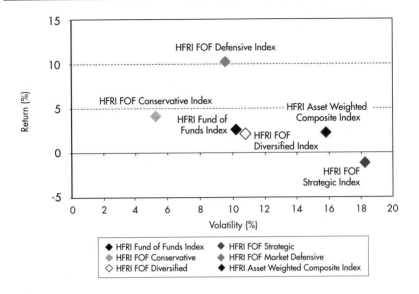

allocations to underlying hedge fund strategies that have low, no, or negative correlation to equity markets. This change in leadership will happen over time as financial markets present different opportunities.

Figure 5-15 summarizes performance for fund of funds and market indices on a yearly basis.

FUND OF FUNDS RISK-ADJUSTED RETURNS—THE SHARPE RATIO

Another statistical measure often used to compare the risk-adjusted returns of the HFRI Fund of Funds Index to the equity and bond market indices is the Sharpe Ratio. The Sharpe Ratio is calculated by dividing the return, adjusted by the risk-free rate (usually 5 percent annually), by the volatility. This ratio indicates in a simplistic fashion the unit of return achieved for one unit of risk. The higher the number is, the more return was achieved for the risk taken.

Figure 5-15 FOF Performance Compared With Traditional Indices and Hedge Fund Composite

(%)	Traditional			Alternative Investment Strategies	
	Equities		Bonds	HFRI Asset Weighted Composite Index	HFR Fund of Funds Index
	MSCI World	S&P 500	Lehman Govt/Credit		
1990	-18.66	-3.09	10.40	11.75	17.53
1991	15.99	30.40	20.29	42.13	14.50
1992	-7.14	7.60	9.22	26.21	12.33
1993	20.38	10.05	13.20	50.07	26.32
1994	3.34	1.32	-4.13	-1.92	-3.48
1995	18.70	37.54	22.74	26.26	11.10
1996	11.73	22.92	3.35	14.21	14.39
1997	14.16	33.33	9.87	18.01	16.20
1998	22.79	28.59	12.00	4.36	-5.11
1999	23.54	21.03	-2.40	29.11	26.47
2000	-14.07	-9.09	13.27	1.87	4.07
2001	-17.83	-11.85	9.39	4.75	2.80
2002	-21.06	-22.33	12.09	-0.32	1.01
ROR					
1990–02*	2.60	9.65	9.70	16.39	10.19
2000–02*	-17.70	-14.62	11.57	2.08	2.62
Standard Deviation					
1990–02**	15.07	15.26	4.96	8.67	5.94
2000–02**	16.96	18.75	4.39	7.88	5.12
Sharpe Ratio					
1990–02***	-0.09	0.35	0.88	1.23	0.83
2000–02***	-1.35	-1.01	1.39	-0.33	-0.45

All annual returns are total returns in US$.
* Arithmetic average of annual total returns
** Standard deviation of annual returns
*** Sharpe ratio. 5% is used as risk-free rate.

SHARPE RATIO 1990–2002

During the period from 1990 to 2002 the HFRI Fund of Funds Index had a Sharpe Ratio higher than equity market indices and comparable to bonds. As shown in *Figure 5-16*, the Sharpe Ratio for the HFRI Fund of Funds Index was 0.87, beating both the S&P 500 and MSCI World Indices, which had ratios of 0.31 and -0.16,

Figure 5-16 Rolling One-Year Sharpe Ratio, January 1991–December 2002

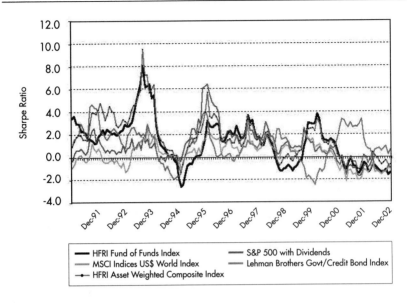

Figure 5-17 Rolling One-Year Sharpe Ratio, January 1991–December 2002

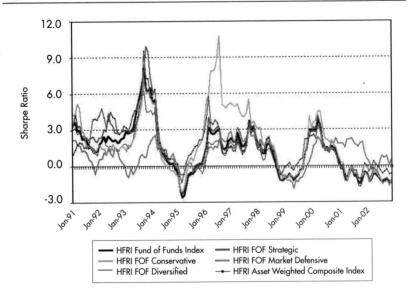

respectively, and comparable to bonds at 0.95. The highest Sharpe Ratio, however, was achieved by the HFRI Asset Weighted Composite Index at 1.23.

At the substrategy level, illustrated in *Figure 5-17*, the HFRI Fund of Funds: Conservative Index had the highest Sharpe ratio for the entire period at 1.18. This figure is higher than the bond index, indicating that funds of funds can achieve higher risk-adjusted returns than bonds. The Sharpe ratios for the HFRI Fund of Funds: Strategic Index, HFRI Fund of Funds: Diversified Index, and HFRI Fund of Funds: Market Defensive indices were, respectively, 0.89, 0.68, and 0.91.

SHARPE RATIO 2000–2002

In the more recent period, as shown in *Figure 5-18*, the Sharpe ratios are less meaningful, with all but the Lehman Bond Index in negative territory[1], indicating the relative strength of the bond markets since 2001.

Figure 5-18   Rolling One-Year Sharpe Ratio, January 2000–December 2002

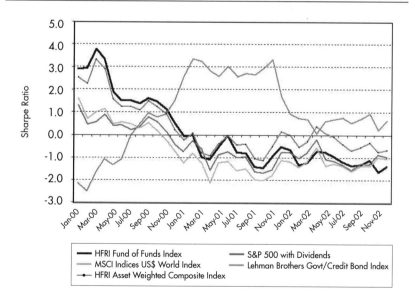

Figure 5-19 Rolling One-Year Sharpe Ratio, January 2000–December 2002

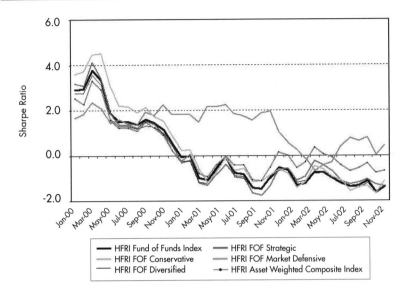

At the substrategy level, *Figure 5-19* reveals that only the HFRI Fund of Funds: Market Defensive Index achieved a positive Sharpe ratio for the more recent period.

PRESERVATION OF CAPITAL 1990–2002

FUND OF FUNDS PERFORMANCE VERSUS EQUITIES

When comparing the largest losing period for funds of funds to that for equities it is apparent that the magnitude of losses has historically been much less for funds of funds than for equities. The largest one-month loss for the HFRI Fund of Funds Index was -7.5 percent compared with -7.37 for HFRI Asset Weighted Composite, –14.4 percent for the S&P 500, and –13.5 percent for the MSCI World. Reviewing the worst twelve-month return, the HFRI Asset Weighted Composite Index is the better relative performer, with a loss of only 5.13 percent, compared with losses for the HFRI Funds of Funds Index, the S&P 500, and

MSCI World Indices of 7.00, 26.6 percent, and 29.05 percent, respectively.

FUND OF FUNDS PERFORMANCE DURING BEAR AND BULL MARKETS

Historically, funds of funds have outperformed the equity markets during bear markets. Compared with the MSCI World Index, the HFRI Fund of Funds Index had its largest outperformance in 1990, when the MSCI World Index was down 18.66 percent and the HFRI Fund of Funds Index was up more than 17 percent. The worst under-performance was in 1998, when the MSCI World Index was up 22.79 percent and the HFRI Fund of Funds Index was down more than 5 percent. More recently, during the bear markets of 2000, 2001, and 2002, funds of funds continued to outperform. (See *Figure 5-20*.)

When comparing the HFRI Fund of Funds Index to the S&P 500, this same trend is evident. In 1990, the S&P was down more than 3 percent, underperforming the HFRI Fund of Funds Index by 20.62 percent. But in 1998, funds of funds underperformed the S&P 500 by 33.7 percent.

Figure 5-20 S&P Drawdown From Peak

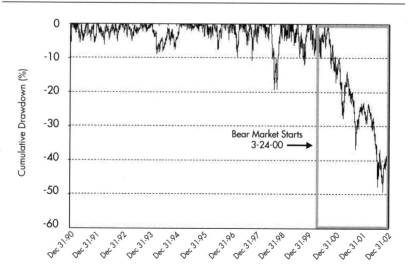

Figure 5-21 Average Negative Versus Positive Returns, 1990–2002

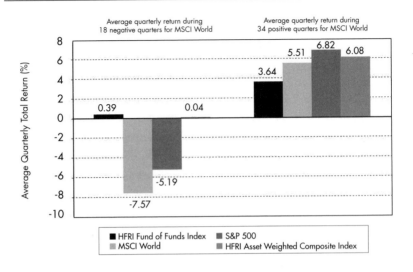

Figure 5-22 Average Negative Versus Positive Returns, 2000–2002

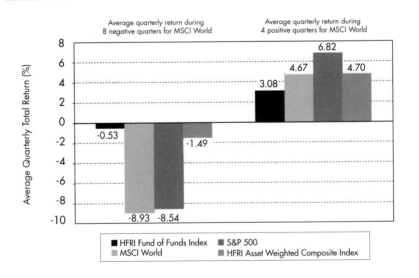

AVERAGE PERFORMANCE DURING NEGATIVE PERIODS AND POSITIVE PERIODS 1990–2002

As illustrated in *Figure 5-21*, the MSCI World Index had eighteen quarters since 1990 (out of a total of fifty-two) of negative returns, with an average decline of 7.57 percent. During these same eighteen quarters, the average return for the HFRI Fund of Funds Index was positive 0.39 percent. The average return for the S&P 500 during these quarters was –5.19 percent. HFRI Asset Weighted Composite remained neutral with a 0.04 percent gain.

On the positive side, the MSCI World Index recorded thirty-four gaining quarters for which the average return was 5.51 percent. During the same quarters the average return for the S&P 500 was 6.82 percent, while the HFRI Fund of Funds Index returned 3.64 percent. The HFRI Asset Weighted Composite performed more strongly than funds of funds, gaining 6.08 percent.

These data support the expectation that funds of funds provide asset protection in the event of an equity market downturn, while posting positive returns in up equity markets. The relationships are even more pronounced in the more recent period of stock market decline, as seen in *Figure 5-22*.

Figure 5-23 provides the numerical data used in several of the preceding charts and graphs.

RETURN DISTRIBUTION 1990–2002

By overlaying the actual distribution of returns for the HFRI Fund of Funds Index on the implied normal distribution for the MSCI World Index (the actual distribution for the MSCI World is very close to normal for this time period), and the normal distribution implied by the HFRI Fund of Funds returns, we can make several observations about the character of fund of funds returns.

As *Figure 5-24* shows, the monthly returns for the HFRI Fund of Funds Index form a peaked distribution by comparison with the MSCI distribution. Additionally, there is a high frequency of returns between 0 percent and 5 percent, indicating the ability of funds of

Figure 5-23   Fund of Hedge Funds Risk and Return Characteristics

	# of monthly returns*	Annual return (%)	Volatility (%)	Sharpe ratio**	Worst 1-month return (%)	Negative months	Worst 12-month return (%)
S&P 500	156	9.65	15.26	0.55	-14.44	59	-26.59
MSCI World	156	2.60	15.07	-0.09	-13.45	66	-29.05
Lehman Brothers Govt/Credit	156	9.70	4.96	0.89	-2.87	44	-5.44
HFRI Asset Weighted Composite	156	16.39	8.67	1.23	-7.37	43	-5.13
HFRI Fund of Funds Index	156	10.19	5.94	0.83	-7.47	42	-7.44

* January 1990 to December 2002
** Based on risk-free rate of 5%

funds to deliver positive returns with lower volatility. Lastly, the funds of funds' returns have a fat negative tail, that is, the magnitude of the worst return is more than would be indicated by a normal distribution. The cost, it would seem, of the general low volatility of funds of funds' returns is an occasional outlier to the negative side.

FUND OF FUNDS PERFORMANCE DURING PERIODS OF MARKET STRESS

Systemic events, those crises that place the markets and the functioning of the markets themselves under severe strain, also bear analysis, to see how funds of funds weathered difficult periods in the financial markets. The 1990s and early 2000s saw four major financial crises. The HFRI Fund of Funds Index outperformed the S&P 500 in three out of the last four equity market crises. The notable exception was the Russian debt crises in 1998 during which the HFRI Fund of Funds Index was down more than 11 percent. This can be explained by a combination of factors. First, the generally optimistic period that preceded the crisis left many managers exposed to the equity markets. Second, the hedge fund industry had a significant exposure to Russian debt and other emerging markets.

Figure 5-24 Rolling Distribution, January 1990–December 2002

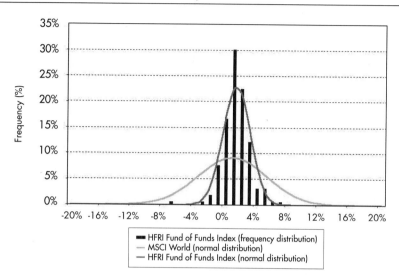

The subsequent liquidity crisis during the period caused a rapid re-valuation of risk premia, causing losses for all strategies that hedged investments in riskier assets with investment in similar but less risky assets. This problem was compounded by the forced liquidation of one of the largest hedge funds, the much written about demise of Long-Term Capital Management[2]. The liquidation of LTCM's portfolio directly impacted managers running similar strategies. The worst-performing strategies during the crisis were Equity Hedge, Emerging Markets, and Fixed Income Arbitrage. However, it can be said that fund of funds managers, and the hedge fund managers they invest with, learned from their experiences, given the relative strength of returns during subsequent financial crises.

SUMMARY

The flow of assets into funds of funds is supported by their absolute and relative performance, as discussed in this chapter. Overall, funds of funds have generated more stable and consistent returns than the stock market. This has been accomplished not by generating larger returns than stocks, but by way of more consistent returns and smaller losses during down periods. Because of this, the compounded return of funds of funds beat stocks on a risk-adjusted basis. While it appears that a rapidly rising equity market will tend to outperform funds of funds, their performance in the period since March 2000 has demonstrated their ability to preserve capital and generate positive returns even when equity markets are posting large losses. All in all, funds of funds are a lower-risk investment than stocks, able to generate similar long-term results with a fraction of the volatility. By comparison with the hedge fund industry as a whole, funds of funds as a group have underperformed over the long term. In the more recent period, the average funds of funds performance has tracked more closely to hedge fund index performance. As in all fields of investing, it is difficult to consistently outperform the market after active management fees.

Chapter Notes

1. The Sharpe ratio calculation breaks down as a measure of risk-adjusted returns when negative returns are involved. For example, a strategy that returns –10 percent with 15 percent volatility would have a Sharpe ratio of –1.0, while a strategy returning –10 percent with 5 percent volatility would have a Sharpe ratio of –3.0.

2. For more on the demise of Long-Term Capital Management, see Roger Lowenstein's *When Genius Failed: The Rise and Fall of Long-Term Capital Management* (Random House, 2001) and Nicholas Dunbar's *Inventing Money: The Story of Long-Term Capital Management and the Legends Behind It* (John Wiley & Sons, 2000).

Fund of Funds in a Portfolio With Traditional Assets

6

A s ILLUSTRATED IN Chapter 5, funds of funds (FOFs) offer competitive returns with volatility lower than that of traditional long-only investments in equities, and similar to that of bonds. In addition, they have low correlation to traditional investments in stocks and bonds. Both of these characteristics allow investors to improve risk-adjusted returns by diversifying a portion of a traditional portfolio of stocks and bonds into low correlation fund of funds strategies. This chapter examines performance results that would have been obtained historically by adding a fund of funds investment to a traditional portfolio of stocks and bonds. Linear regression analysis and mean-variance optimization are employed to illustrate the point.

LINEAR ANALYSIS OF RETURNS

A common way of examining a series of returns is by comparing the returns with those of a benchmark. The most common method is to compare them to a proxy for an asset class, such as the S&P 500 for U.S. equities. Using traditional linear regression analysis we can determine the relationship between the returns generated by a fund of funds (the dependent variable) and the market return (the independent variable). The relationship is described by the regression line that is the best linear fit between the two streams of returns. The equation of the line takes the form y = a + bx, where y is the expected fund of funds return, a is alpha (the y-intercept), b is beta (the slope of the line), and x is the market return.

There are three important indications produced through linear regression analysis. First, this analysis produces a correlation statistic, referred to as r, which indicates the direction and strength of the relationship between the two streams of returns. Thus, a correlation of 1 would indicate that the fund of funds returns are completely determined by the market returns, without error. Second, beta indicates the magnitude of that relationship, and is generally accepted as a proxy for systemic market risk. For example, a beta of 2.0 indicates that for a 1 percent increase in the stock market return we would expect the portion of the strategy return explained by market return (as indicated by the correlation statistic) to increase by 2 percent. Lastly, alpha indicates the residual portion of the expected strategy return that is unexplained by fluctuations in the stock market return. It is widely accepted as a measure of the value added through active portfolio management.

As indicated in *Figure 6-1*, which compares fund of funds performance with selected market and hedge fund indices, funds of funds as a group tend to have moderate-to-low correlation and low betas relative to the stock market. Thus, their returns are largely independent of stock market fluctuations. The portion of the return unexplained by stock market fluctuations, alpha, should be highlighted. Although alpha is commonly thought of as a reflection of management skill, it should be emphasized that some portion is attributable to the strategy itself. Funds of funds invest in underlying hedge funds that pursue strategies that are designed to take advantage of pricing inefficiencies in financial markets. As a result, they are inherently alpha-oriented.

When determining whether a fund of funds should be added to a mix of assets, it is important first to determine whether the asset will add value from a diversification standpoint. Adding a new in-

Figure 6-1   Statistical Profiles, January 1990–December 2002

Strategy	Monthly Average	Monthly Standard Deviation	Correlation to S&P 500	Beta to S&P 500	Alpha S&P 500
S&P 500	0.869	4.407	1.000	1.000	0.000
HFRI Convertible Arbitrage	0.927	0.976	0.325	0.072	0.864
HFRI Distressed Securities	1.139	1.835	0.374	0.156	1.003
HFRI Emerging Markets	1.162	4.542	0.566	0.584	0.655
HFRI Equity Hedge	1.438	2.701	0.655	0.401	1.089
HFRI Equity Market Neutral	0.825	0.946	0.119	0.026	0.803
HFRI Event Driven	1.135	1.984	0.629	0.283	0.889
HFRI Fixed Income Arbitrage	0.698	1.334	-0.068	-0.021	0.716
HFRI Fixed Income MBS Arbitrage*	0.837	1.410	0.021	0.007	0.831
HFRI Fund of Funds	**0.826**	**1.714**	**0.425**	**0.165**	**0.683**
HFRI Macro	1.337	2.528	0.381	0.219	1.147
HFRI Merger Arbitrage	0.892	1.294	0.460	0.135	0.775
HFRI Relative Value Arbitrage	1.034	1.098	0.350	0.087	0.958
HFRI Short Selling	0.519	6.569	-0.696	-1.037	1.420
Lehman Brothers Govt/Credit Bond	0.784	1.432	0.173	0.056	0.736

Data in % except correlation and beta
* Data only available starting 1/1993

vestment class can add value if it has low, no, or negative correlation to the other assets in the portfolio. As was noted, the table above clearly shows that funds of funds have moderate-to-low correlation to the equity markets, represented by the S&P 500. This indicates that the returns for funds of funds are largely independent of stock market returns. That portion of returns unexplained by the stock market is indicated by alpha, which reflects, along with manager skill, also the portion of returns attributable to a strategy or combination of strategies. In this case, the monthly alpha for the fund of funds is 0.68 percent. It should also be noted that although the returns for the fund of fund index are largely independent of the market, there still exists some systemic or market risk, as measured by beta. In this case, the beta for the fund of funds index is 0.165. By adding a fund of funds portfolio to a traditional set of asset classes, volatility and market risk can be reduced without a corresponding reduction in returns. This surprising fact is only possible because market inefficiencies exist and hedge fund managers utilize strategies designed to exploit those inefficiencies.

ADDING FUNDS OF FUNDS TO A TRADITIONAL PORTFOLIO

The riskiness (variance in returns) of a portfolio depends on the correlation among its holdings rather than the average variance of its separate components. Thus, adding an allocation that is highly correlated to an existing portfolio will not generally reduce overall portfolio volatility, because it will move in lockstep with the existing contents. On the other hand, adding a low correlation allocation, particularly one, such as a fund of funds, that exhibits low volatility as a stand-alone investment, can reduce overall portfolio volatility. The idea is to make allocations to strategies that will perform well in different market environments.

Figure 6-2 details the correlation of major hedge fund strategies to the HFRI Fund of Funds Index, the S&P 500, and the Lehman Brothers Government/Credit Bond Index, as well as to each other.

As illustrated in the table, adding an individual hedge fund to a portfolio of traditional assets will lower the portfolio's volatility due to the hedge fund's low correlation with the equity and bond markets, relatively low intrinsic volatility, and consistent ability to

Figure 6-2   Correlation Matrix of Hedge Fund Strategies, Fund of Funds, S&P 500, and Bonds, January 1990–December 2002

	S&P 500	CA	DS	EM	EH	EMN
S&P 500	1.00					
HFRI Convertible Arbitrage	0.32	1.00				
HFRI Distressed Securities	0.37	0.59	1.00			
HFRI Emerging Markets	0.57	0.44	0.64	1.00		
HFRI Equity Hedge	0.66	0.47	0.58	0.64	1.00	
HFRI Equity Market Neutral	0.12	0.14	0.18	0.07	0.34	1.00
HFRI Event Driven	0.63	0.62	0.78	0.69	0.76	0.20
HFRI Fixed Income Arbitrage	-0.07	0.11	0.36	0.27	0.06	0.06
HFRI Fixed Income MBS Arbitrage*	0.02	0.17	0.31	0.21	0.09	0.14
HFRI Fund of Funds	**0.42**	**0.48**	**0.58**	**0.73**	**0.75**	**0.32**
HFRI Macro	0.38	0.39	0.46	0.60	0.58	0.23
HFRI Merger Arbitrage	0.46	0.46	0.52	0.42	0.46	0.18
HFRI Relative Value Arbitrage	0.35	0.56	0.70	0.49	0.52	0.21
HFRI Short Selling	-0.70	-0.36	-0.47	-0.57	-0.79	-0.11
Lehman Brothers Govt/Credit Bond	0.17	0.19	0.04	0.01	0.09	0.21

* Data only available starting 1/1993

deliver alpha versus traditional market measures. Developing this relationship further, the addition of several hedge funds with low cross-correlation, through a fund of funds, can reduce risk in a portfolio of traditional investments.

Since a fund of funds will invest pooled assets into other hedge funds, it is important to understand the relationship between the underlying strategies. With returns derived from widely differing strategies, one would expect little correlation between the strategies. The highest strategy-to-strategy correlation exists between Event Driven and Distressed Securities at 0.78. Intuitively, this is not surprising given that many Event Driven managers use Distressed Securities as a core component of their multi-strategy approach. The strategies with lowest correlation to the rest of the strategies are Short Selling, Fixed Income Arbitrage, and Equity Market Neutral, with the average off-diagonal correlations -0.41, 0.14, and 0.17 respectively.

Modern portfolio theory, or MPT, uses quantitative models to maximize output given a certain level of input, or, alternatively, to minimize input given a certain desired level of output. The result of the model is what has come to be called an "efficient frontier," or

ED	FIA	FIMBSA	FOF	M	MA	RVA	SS	BONDS
1.00								
0.17	1.00							
0.22	0.52	1.00						
0.64	**0.25**	**0.27**	**1.00**					
0.55	0.12	0.22	0.71	1.00				
0.73	-0.02	0.02	0.34	0.28	1.00			
0.64	0.30	0.21	0.48	0.37	0.43	1.00		
-0.63	-0.03	-0.03	-0.50	-0.40	-0.37	-0.38	1.00	
0.08	-0.21	0.03	0.09	0.36	0.09	0.04	-0.02	1.00

the set of possible portfolio allocations that maximize expected returns for a given level of variance (risk), or minimize variance (risk) for a given level of return. The model reveals the mathematical appeal of diversification. Modern portfolio theory provides some interesting insights into asset allocations that include stocks, bonds, and funds of funds.

Funds of funds invest in strategies that derive returns from relationships between securities rather than the directional bias associated with traditional investments in stocks or bonds. And while those relationships are subject to volatility, as a group the returns they have produced over the past decade generally have been more stable than, and have had low correlation to, traditional stock and bond indices. This point is illustrated in *Figure 6-3* using modern portfolio theory.[1]

For each level of risk (standard deviation) the efficient frontier maximizes historical returns given the allocation options (funds of funds, stocks, bonds). All of the points on the curve represent

Figure 6-3 Efficient Frontier: Fund of Hedge Funds
          January 1990–December 2002

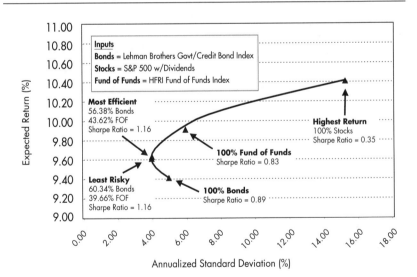

"efficient portfolios," meaning they maximize expected return for a given level of variance, or they minimize variance for a given level of return. No combination of assets can be put together to yield a result to the left of the curve. The set of all possible allocations, including one of 100 percent to bonds and one of 100 percent to stocks, resides on or inside the frontier. The most efficient allocation is that allocation with the highest risk-adjusted return as measured by the Sharpe ratio.

In this case, the most efficient allocation would be made up of an allocation of roughly 44 percent to the HFRI Fund of Funds Index and 56 percent to bonds. This is to be expected since the HFRI Fund of Funds Index is an aggregate of funds of funds, which in turn invests in multiple hedge fund strategies, which invest in a wide range of uncorrelated asset classes.

The graph is not necessarily a recommendation to invest 44 percent of a portfolio in a single or multiple funds of funds. However, the benefits to diversifying using this asset class cannot be overlooked.

Figure 6-4 shows how overall portfolio volatility is reduced by adding funds of funds to a traditional portfolio of stocks and bonds in 10 percent increments. The result is striking, indicated by the low slope of the line. Although volatility is being reduced, there is not a corresponding reduction in return. In fact, as funds of funds are added to a traditional portfolio, the risk-adjusted returns, as measured by the Sharpe Ratio, increase. It is important to note that the proportion of stocks and bonds remains fixed at 60/40 (e.g., 20 percent funds of funds, 48 percent stocks, and 32 percent bonds).

In other words, by adding a fund of funds investment to a traditional portfolio of stocks and bonds, volatility could be reduced without a commensurate decrease in return.

As we have seen, returns generated by a traditional portfolio can be enhanced on a risk-adjusted basis by allocating a portion of the investment capital to a fund of funds. Additionally, such an allocation can reduce systemic market risk as measured by beta. A traditional portfolio of stocks and bonds, in a 60/40 mix, would have returned approximately 10 percent since 1990. The stock

Figure 6-4 Improvement in Sharpe Ratio by Adding Fund of Funds to a 60/40
Portfolio of Stocks/Bonds, January 1990–December 2002

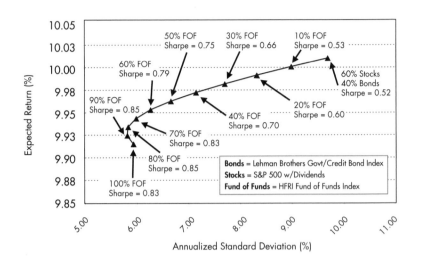

Figure 6-5 Fund of Funds as Alternative to Bonds I
January 1990–December 2002

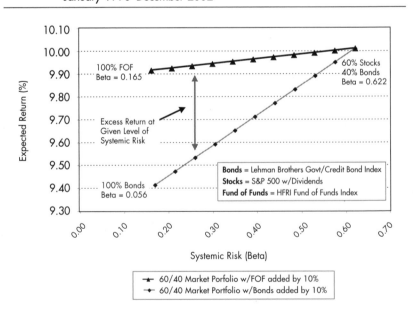

market beta for this portfolio over the same time period would have been 0.62. When funds of funds are added to this traditional mix in 10 percent increments (e.g., 20 percent funds of funds, 48 percent stocks, and 32 percent bonds), market risk is reduced while at the same time maintaining competitive portfolio returns. At each level of the systemic risk incurred, the portfolio with an allocation to the market-neutral strategies offers higher returns than the portfolio consisting of stocks and bonds only. *Figure 6-5* shows that increasing the allocation to bonds reduces systemic risk, but it does so at a greater cost to returns than if the allocation to funds of funds is increased while holding the stock/bond mix constant at 60/40. At any level to the left of the traditional 60/40 portfolio mix, a combination of funds of funds with the traditional mix produces a superior risk-to-return profile for the combined portfolio. The combined portfolio return is reduced by 0.9 percent along this sample of portfolios. However, market risk, as measured by beta, is reduced by over 70 percent.

The Treynor Measure is another methodology by which to illustrate that the return-to-risk ratio attributes produced by combining funds of funds with the traditional portfolio mix are superior to those of the traditional portfolio. The Treynor Measure is similar to the Sharpe Ratio, but replaces variance with beta in the denominator. *Figure 6-6* illustrates that as exposure to stock market risk is reduced by adding a larger allocation to funds of funds, beta declines at a faster rate than the combined portfolio return, which in turn results in a strong upward movement in the Treynor Measure.

Additionally, the rate at which the Treynor Measure improves (as beta is reduced for the combined portfolio) is much higher than if the bond allocation were to be increased. It may be possible for investors to achieve returns similar to those of the traditional portfolio mix by adding a fund of funds investment while at the same time reducing exposure to systemic market risk.

Similar results occur when a traditional stock/bond portfolio is compared to a stock/fund of funds portfolio. *Figure 6-7* shows the two sets of returns at a given level of systemic risk. The lower line is the traditional mix of stocks and bonds; the upper line replaces

Figure 6-6   Rise in Treynor Measure as Fund of Funds is Substituted for Bonds
January 1990–December 2002

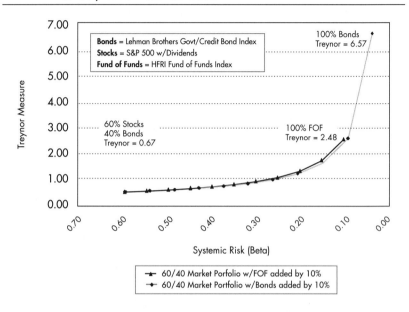

Figure 6-7   Fund of Funds as Alternative to Bonds II
January 1990–December 2002

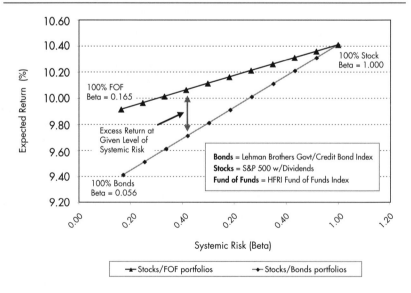

bonds with an investment in a fund of funds index. As the graph shifts to the right, the allocation to stocks decreases in 10 percent increments. As illustrated in the figure, the portfolio consisting of any combination of stocks with an allocation to a fund of funds provides better return/risk characteristics than the stock and bond portfolio allocations.

Since 1990, the S&P 500 has posted an average annual return of 11.26 percent, which, of course, is accompanied by a beta of 1. The Lehman Brothers Government/Credit Bond Index has posted returns on average of 9.41 percent with a beta to the stock market of 0.17. Traditionally, investors would use an allocation of bonds to diversify equity market exposure and reduce portfolio volatility. However, by replacing bonds with funds of funds, investors may be able to achieve higher returns at a given level of stock market risk.

Using the Treynor Measure, *Figure 6-8* indicates that a portfolio of stocks with an allocation to funds of funds produces comparable returns to a portfolio of stocks and bonds. As before, as the graph shifts to the right, the allocation to stocks decreases by 10 percent

Figure 6-8　Rise in Treynor Measure as Fund of Funds is Substituted for Bonds January 1990–December 2002

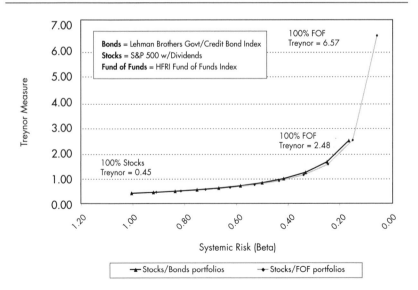

incrementally from 100 to 0 percent. Additionally, the rate at which the Treynor Measure improves as beta is reduced for the combined portfolio of stocks and funds of funds is higher than that of the stock and bond portfolio. Therefore, by replacing the allocation of bonds with an allocation to funds of funds in a traditional stock/bond portfolio, significantly higher risk-adjusted returns may be attained.

ACHIEVING SUPERIOR RISK-ADJUSTED RETURNS

The analysis of returns demonstrates that an allocation to funds of funds can improve the risk-adjusted returns of a traditional portfolio of stocks and bonds. It is precisely these performance characteristics that have caused funds of funds to be increasingly incorporated into portfolio allocations of institutions and individuals alike. With the case for funds of funds thus made, we will proceed in Part 3 of the book to lay out a commonsense approach to evaluating and selecting a fund of funds.

SUMMARY

Funds of funds offer competitive returns with lower volatility than traditional long-only investments in equities, and comparable to bonds. In addition, they have low correlation to traditional investments in stocks and bonds. Both of these characteristics allow investors to improve risk-adjusted returns by diversifying a portion of a traditional portfolio of stocks and bonds into low correlation fund of funds strategies. Adding a low correlation allocation to an existing portfolio of stocks and bonds, particularly one, such as a fund of funds, that exhibits low volatility as a stand-alone investment, can reduce overall portfolio volatility without a commensurate fall in returns. The idea is to make allocations to strategies that will perform well in different market environments. The analysis of returns in this chapter demonstrates that an allocation to funds of funds can improve the risk-adjusted returns of a traditional portfolio of stocks and bonds. It is precisely these performance characteristics that have caused funds of funds to be increasingly incorporated into portfolio allocations from institutions and individuals alike.

Chapter Note

1. Efficient frontier calculations involve optimizations and use average monthly returns (versus geometric average returns used in the historical statistics tables and charts in previous chapters). For volatile return streams the simple average tends to be much higher than the geometric average because geometric average takes compounding into effect. This is why return for the S&P 500 index in Figure 6-3 is higher than that of Figure 5-11. The following is a comparison table for geometric and arithmetic monthly averages.

Monthly Arithmetic Versus Geometric Average Returns
January 1990–December 2002

Index	Arithmetic	Geometric
S&P 500	0.87%	0.77%
Lehman Brothers	0.78%	0.77%
HFRI FOF	0.83%	0.81%

Since the S&P 500 index exhibited the highest volatility for the period considered, it shows the largest difference between the two returns.

PART 3

A Commonsense Approach to Selecting Funds of Funds

Defining Objectives and Identifying Candidates 7

F UNDS OF FUNDS OFFER a range of return expectations, different structural features, and varied approaches to portfolio management. Investors need a process to sort and weigh the many options in order to find the fund of funds that best fits their requirements. The first step in this process is defining fund of funds investment objectives and parameters. The investment objectives are the goals, or desired investment results, of the funds of funds investment. The parameters set forth the path to be taken in the attempt to reach the goals.

Defining investment objectives and parameters helps an investor to (1) establish realistic goals and expectations for a fund of funds investment, (2) have focused search criteria with which to narrow the field of potential fund of funds candidates, and (3) serve as an ongoing evaluation framework for a fund of funds investment once it has been made.

STEP 1: DEFINE OBJECTIVES AND PARAMETERS

OBJECTIVES

Objectives are what the investor seeks to achieve through the fund of funds investment. These can include performance, volatility, maximum drawdown, and correlation targets. An investor, for example, may have the following long-term objectives for the fund of funds investment:

- 10 percent annualized net return (after all manager and fund of funds fees)
- annualized standard deviation of less than 8 percent
- maximum peak-to-valley loss of 7 percent
- correlation of less than 0.5 to global equity markets

An investor may have other goals, such as outperformance of a selected benchmark (a traditional index, a broad hedge fund index, a combination of hedge fund strategy indices representing the strategy set the fund of funds limits its selection to, or a peer group of funds of funds pursuing approaches similar to that of the investor's fund of funds).

Many investors also use absolute return targets as a goal. For example, if an investor sets an absolute return target of 10 percent annually, then the fund of funds investment would be evaluated against this fixed goal. This approach has emerged in response to the "absolute return" concept whereby hedge funds are purported to be able to maintain consistent levels of returns independent of market conditions and cycles. This notion is more a marketing myth than reality, however.

All hedge fund strategies have a relationship to, and are therefore "relative" to, one or a combination of markets or market factors, long or short, which will affect the level of returns available to the strategies. Therefore, the use of hedge fund strategy indices creates a more realistic benchmark. Under some market conditions, many hedge fund strategies perform well; during others, only a few will meet expectations. Because of this unpredictability, even though a fund of funds can shift among strategies, it may not be able to generate absolute return targets without sacrificing risk management parameters. A more reasonable target would be a return level linked to the available hedge fund investment opportunities or the risk-free rate.

In setting goals, investors may also consider the source of the assets being allocated. Are the assets to be invested in the fund of funds being moved from equities or bond allocations? If so, an "opportunity cost" approach may be taken, which measures the excess returns generated by the fund of funds relative to the traditional investments.

PARAMETERS

Parameters are constraints that define the universe of funds of funds available for investment and govern the investor's search. A fund of funds that meets the established parameters may be considered for investment; a fund of funds that falls outside of the constraints is eliminated from the pool of investment choices. Parameters can be thought of as the "rules of the game," and can be separated into two groups: strategy restrictions and structural requirements.

Parameters may be driven by regulatory requirements and limitations, internal requirements, or risk guidelines specific to hedge fund investing. For example, these might include restrictions on the use of leverage, futures, or non-OECD investments. (The OECD, or Organization for Economic Cooperation and Development, sets guidelines for international investments.) They may include strategy and manager diversification requirements. Other parameters might include fee levels and liquidity provisions. Tax treatment is another possible parameter. A taxable investor might require a fund of funds where tax consequences pass through to the investor, whereas a tax-exempt investor would look for a structure that blocks the pass-through of certain tax consequences. A sample of some strategy restrictions and structural requirements are set forth below.

STRATEGY RESTRICTIONS

Strategy restrictions limit how the fund of funds or its underlying hedge funds can invest. The following examples illustrate typical restrictions:

- Minimum number of managers in fund of funds: twenty
- Maximum allocation per individual manager: 8 percent of net asset value (NAV)
- Minimum of five investment strategies in the fund of funds, and not more than 30 percent of NAV in any one strategy
- Maximum of 5 percent of NAV invested in securities markets of emerging market countries
- Maximum of 2 percent of NAV invested in illiquid securities (securities for which a secondary market does not exist at all times)
- Maximum leverage of fund of funds: three times gross exposure
- Length of fund of funds track record: four years

STRUCTURAL REQUIREMENTS

Structural requirements deal with the investment terms and level of service offered by a fund of funds, such as liquidity provisions, transparency, reporting, and risk management. These might be general, such as requirements for quarterly liquidity and monthly reporting, or more specific, such as daily risk management and independent pricing. Of course, the objectives and parameters must relate to what is available in the markets. For example, while one may like to invest in a fund of funds that will never have a losing month and has daily liquidity, if none exist, it is not a useful goal and parameter to work from. Structural requirements might include the following:

- **Liquidity:** Quarterly on not more than 30-days' notice
- **Transparency:** As to strategy allocation and manager concentration
- **Reporting:** Monthly letter with detail on strategy and manager performance

■ **Risk Management:** Daily risk monitoring of fund of funds and manager positions

The worksheet on pages 128–130 can be used to determine the priority and to assess the reasonableness of desired objectives and parameters. An investor may want to develop a more or less comprehensive worksheet, but the purpose of the exercise is to develop solid goals and realistic expectations for the fund of funds investment. With objectives and parameters defined, the investor is ready to screen the universe of funds of funds to identify a short list of funds that are likely to achieve the objectives within the parameters.

STEP 2: SCREEN TO CREATE A FUNDS OF FUNDS SHORT LIST

The screening process begins with a universe comprised of hundreds of funds of funds. Through a series of categorizations, screens, and rankings both quantitative and qualitative, this highly varied multitude of funds of funds is reduced to a short list of candidates that meets, as closely as possible, the criteria established by the investor in setting out objectives and parameters.

The goal of the screening process is to identify one or more funds of funds that are within the established parameters and have a high probability of achieving the stated investment goals. This can be described as a best-fit matching of investor needs and objectives with the available fund of funds opportunities.

While investors should establish their goals and objectives prior to making a fund of funds selection, this may be difficult to do without examining the characteristics and features offered. As a starting point, we group the funds of funds tracked by HFR in four subcategories based on general characteristics. These categories are: HFRI Fund of Funds Conservative Index, HFRI Fund of Funds Strategic Index, HFRI Fund of Funds Diversified Index, and the HFRI Fund of Funds Market Defensive Index. The following are brief descriptions of the subcategories:

Fund of Funds Objectives and Parameters Worksheet

I. RETURN EXPECTATIONS

Long-term return expectations (over the term of a business cycle, approximately five to ten years, or the term of the Fund): _____

_____

Maximum acceptable loss parameter:
Month: _____
Quarter: _____
Year: _____

Minimum acceptable return parameter:
Quarter: _____
Year: _____

Importance of consistency of the Fund's return to the investor:
Not important _____   Relatively important _____
Important _____   Very important _____

Minimum acceptable number of positive return months in a year: _____

_____

Maximum acceptable number of consecutive months of negative performance: _____

Expected long-term volatility of the Fund (annualized standard deviation):

_____

Range: _____
High: _____

II. CORRELATION EXPECTATIONS

Expected long-term correlation to a specific asset class (e.g., S&P 500):

_____

Define specific correlation: _____

_____

Low _____   Medium _____   High _____

Importance to the investor that correlation remains during times of extreme market environments (e.g., when the broad equity markets are up or down more than 15 percent during a quarter/year):
Not very important _____   Relatively important _____
Important _____   Very important _____

Investor expectation of Fund performance in a given quarter/year if broad market returns are negative:

Negative _____   Flat_____   Positive_____

III. DIVERSIFICATION

Are there any restrictions on the types of hedge fund strategies used in the Fund?   Yes _____   No _____

If yes, please specify:

_____ Convertible Arbitrage	_____ Distressed Securities
_____ Short Selling	_____ Event Driven
_____ Hedged Equity	_____ Sector
_____ Merger Arbitrage	_____ Macro
_____ Market Neutral	_____ Relative Value

Are there any restrictions on derivatives trading?

If yes, please specify: _____

_____

Restrictions on the max/min percent in a particular strategy: _____

_____

Restrictions on the max/min percent in any one manager: _____

_____

Restrictions on the max/min number of managers in the Fund: _____

_____

Restrictions on geographic location:

U.S.:   _____

Non-U.S.:   _____

  Europe: _____

  Asia: _____

  Emerging Markets: _____

Sector preference:

If yes, please specify: _____

_____

Restrictions on leverage at the Fund level: _____

_____

Restrictions on leverage at the Manager or strategy level: _____

_____

(continued)

Fund of Funds Objectives and Parameters Worksheet *(cont.)*

▬▬▬▬▬▬▬▬▬▬▬▬▬▬▬▬▬▬▬▬▬▬▬▬▬▬▬▬

IV. BENCHMARK

Benchmark(s) against which Fund performance will be measured:

S&P 500 (if other, specify) _____ HFRX Index _____

Peer Group _____ Customized (define) _____

_____

Absolute Return target range: _____

Evaluation of Fund performance versus benchmark will be:

Monthly _____   Quarterly _____

One year _____   Two year _____

Other _____

HFRI FUND OF FUNDS CONSERVATIVE INDEX

Funds of funds that are classified as conservative may exhibit one or more of the following characteristics: The fund of funds seeks consistent returns by primarily investing in funds that engage in what are typically considered more conservative strategies such as Equity Market Neutral, Fixed Income Arbitrage, Merger Arbitrage, Relative Value Arbitrage, and Convertible Arbitrage. The fund of funds exhibits a lower historical annual standard deviation than the HFRI Fund of Funds Index. The fund of funds performs consistently regardless of market conditions.

HFRI FUND OF FUNDS STRATEGIC INDEX

Funds of funds that are classified as strategic may exhibit one or more of the following characteristics: The fund of funds seeks outsized returns by primarily investing in funds that engage in more volatile, opportunistic strategies, often with significant weightings to Emerging Markets, Sector Long/Short, and Equity Hedge. The fund of funds exhibits a greater dispersion of returns and higher volatility compared to the HFRI Fund of Funds Index. The fund of funds outperforms the HFRI Fund of Funds Index in up equity markets and underperforms the Index in down equity markets.

HFRI FUND OF FUNDS DIVERSIFIED INDEX

Funds of funds that are classified as diversified may exhibit one or more of the following characteristics: The fund of funds is highly diversified and invests in a variety of strategies and among multiple managers. The fund of funds has a historical annual return and/or a standard deviation similar to the HFRI Fund of Funds Index. The fund of funds performance correlates closely to the HFRI Fund of Funds Index. The fund of funds shows performance and return distribution similar to the HFRI Fund of Funds Index. The fund of funds preserves capital and/or makes money in down equity markets and posts positive returns in up equity markets.

HFRI FUND OF FUNDS MARKET DEFENSIVE INDEX

Funds of funds that are classified as market defensive may exhibit one or more of the following characteristics: The fund of funds invests significant assets in funds that engage in strategies with negative correlations to equity markets such as short selling and managed futures. The fund of funds has a negative correlation to equity market indices. The fund of funds exhibits higher relative returns during down equity markets than during up equity markets.

In order to conduct a thorough screen an investor must have access to some level of information about the universe of funds of funds. Unlike mutual funds, almost all funds of funds are private investment vehicles. This means that they are not registered with the Securities and Exchange Commission (SEC) for public advertising and distribution. Information about funds of funds is available through (1) hedge fund databases, which collect the information directly from each fund of funds, (2) consultants and investment advisers who have already conducted a screening and due diligence process on some funds of funds, or (3) brokers that offer such products to their clients.

To perform a screen, an investor must build a database of information from various sources or subscribe to an existing database. What kind of information is available in databases? A typical entry may look like that set forth in the following table:

Basic Fund Information

Fund of Funds Name:	**Sample Fund of Funds**
Firm Name:	**Sample Fund Management**
Denomination:	**USD**
Strategy:	**Fund of Funds**
Sub Strategy:	**Low Vol**
Fund Assets:	**$155,000,000**
Date:	**December 31, 2002**
Firm Assets:	**$325,000,000**
Domicile:	**Illinois**
Structure:	**Limited Partnership**
Registration:	**RIA**
Minimum Investment:	**$1,000,000**
Additional Investment:	**$100,000**
Inception Date:	**1/1/98**
OM Date:	**6/99**
Use of Leverage:	**No**
Management Fee:	**1 percent**
Admin Fee:	**0.5 percent**
Incentive Fee:	**10 percent**
Sales Fee:	**0 percent**
Redemption Fee:	**1 percent if less than twelve months**
Other Fees:	**0**
High-Water Mark:	**Yes**
Hurdle Rate:	**No**
Firm Principal(s):	**John Smith**
Investment Information:	
Investor Type:	Accredited U.S. _____
	Qualified U.S. _____
	U.S. Tax-Exempt_____
U.S. Taxable:	**Yes**
U.S. Tax-Exempt:	**Yes**
Non U.S.	**No**
Subscriptions:	**Monthly**
Redemption:	**Quarterly**

Redemption Notice:	**90 days**
Performance Report to Investors:	**Monthly**
Performance Audit:	**12/31**
Accepting New Investments:	**Yes**
Lockup:	**Yes**
Banking Agent:	**Chase Manhattan Bank**
Legal Adviser:	**Seward & Kissel**
Auditors:	**Ernst & Young**
Placement Agent:	**Bermuda Trust**
Administrator:	**Fortis Fund Services Limited**
Custodian:	**Bermuda Trust Limited**
Consultant:	**None**

Strategy Description:
The objectives of the fund is to achieve 10 percent to 14 percent net annualized returns ...

Fund Contact:	**Joe Sample**
Phone:	**312-555-0546**
E-mail:	**joe@sample.com**
Fax:	**312-555-0547**

Management Firm Information:

Founded:	**1998**
Percent of Firm Employee Owned:	**50 percent**
Number of Employees With Ownership Stake:	**10**
Manager Registered as:	**Investment Adviser**
Instrument:	_____
Region:	_____
Industry:	_____
Investor Type:	**20 percent Pension Funds, 35 percent HNW Individuals, 15 percent Institutional, 15 percent Endowments, 15 percent Other**
ROR (Rate of Return):	_____
NAV (Net Asset Value):	_____

The following are brief descriptions of what some of the key data points in the above table mean and what to look for:

Denomination: Most funds of funds are invested using U.S. dollar currency. However, a growing number are denominated in euros and a few in other currencies as well. A U.S. investor investing in a euro-denominated fund will be taking U.S. dollar/euro currency risk.

Strategy: The strategy categorizations are still far from uniform. They can range from an assessment of volatility to a description of the strategy composition, such as "market neutral," "diversified," or "absolute return."

Firm and Fund Assets: It is helpful to understand the relationship between firm assets and fund assets to determine how the firm resource and focus is allocated.

Domicile and Structure: These terms refer to the law under which the fund of funds was formed. Structural forms include limited partnerships, offshore corporations, trusts, limited liability companies, and mutual funds.

Registration: This designation can apply to the fund of funds itself, for example, a mutual fund or registered investment company, or the fund manager who might be registered as an investment adviser or a commodity pool operator.

Minimum Investment: Reference here is to the stated minimum investment. Fund of funds managers usually have the discretion to accept lesser amounts.

Additional Investment: Once an initial investment is made, smaller amounts may be accepted. There are accounting costs associated with such transactions.

Inception Date: This is the date when the fund of funds began doing business. Check this date against the beginning date of the track record to see if data is missing or a pro-forma track record is being presented.

OM Date: The Offering Memorandum is dated and should reflect the latest version as amended. It will not necessarily have a current date unless recently changed. It is worth understanding what changes have been made in relation to the fund's history and performance. For example, if a fund has extended its redemption notice period or incorporated a longer lockup, it may indicate a shift in the investment style toward more illiquid investments.

Use of Leverage: Some funds of funds are authorized to increase their exposure to underlying hedge funds by borrowing money to make additional investments. A fund of funds that leverages "up to 50 percent" can borrow fifty cents for every dollar invested for an investment exposure of 150 percent.

Redemptions: Redemptions are covered in more detail in Chapter 3, but it bears repeating to consider the frequency of redemption (monthly, quarterly, annually) in combination with the notice period (90 days) to understand the actual investment liquidity.

Reporting Frequency: The level of detail and the timing of these reports are not standardized and can vary widely.

Performance Audit: Fund of funds performance audits are based on the audits provided by the underlying hedge funds. Audits are not necessarily a guarantee of the integrity of the performance numbers presented, but they indicate a level of independent review of the fund of funds performance.

Lockup: Lockups will alter the liquidity of the fund of funds investment for some initial period of time. Often an investor can redeem within the lockup period, but will be subject to a fee for doing so. In addition, lockups are an indication of the investment time horizon of underlying investments.

Service Providers: Depending on its structure, a fund of funds will have some combination of these outside professionals. Service providers should be contacted during the due diligence process.

Strategy Description: Strategy descriptions vary widely in terms of detail and useful descriptiveness. In most cases, an independent assessment will be required to arrive at uniform descriptions across managers.

Management Firm Information: The management firm is the entity that operates the fund of funds and is the focus of the evaluation of the asset management capabilities of the fund of funds.

NAV: Net Asset Value is also a way of expressing the performance of a fund of funds. Investors in offshore funds purchase shares at the current NAV share price. It expresses the value of an investment made at the inception of the fund of funds. Usually, the starting amount is $100 or $1,000. Thus, an NAV of 1100 has increased by 10 percent since the inception of the fund. The change between the NAV from one month to the next equates to the monthly rate of return (ROR).

SUMMARY

The general quantitative and qualitative information collected about the funds of funds is screened through the objectives and parameters. Funds of funds without desired characteristics, such as appropriate investment goals, length of track record, fees, or liquidity provision are eliminated from the search. If the initial screening process yields a list of funds of funds still too large to take through the due diligence process, a second elimination level should be conducted using tighter parameters. Often during this process, an increased understanding in the available fund of funds features allows for revisions of the initial objectives and parameters.

The end result of the entire screening process is to arrive at a short list of fund of funds candidates. The funds of funds on this list appear to satisfy the objectives and constraints that have been established and seem to be able to deliver the stated objectives as well. Because the due diligence process is more time consuming and costly, the short list represents the manageable number of funds of funds that an investor can process and evaluate in detail.

Issues in Due Diligence: The Fund of Funds Firm

8

S TRONG, SUSTAINED INVESTMENT performance by a fund of funds is often associated with a well-run business operation. This chapter examines the fund of funds management company as the foundation upon which the fund of funds' portfolio and risk management process is built. The questions discussed are taken from the Alternative Investment Management Association's (AIMA's) Illustrative Questionnaire for Due Diligence of Fund of Funds Managers. (See Appendix A.)

Understanding the history of the firm, its key personnel, business model, sources of revenue, and operating costs are all important factors in determining whether a fund of funds is likely to produce top investment returns going forward. Investors, of course, will want to invest with a firm that has minimal business risk—that is, the risk of disruption in or ceasing operation. But determining the probability of one fund of funds outperforming another often-times depends on a more nuanced analysis of factors such as the financial incentives of the firm's business model, the quality of the firm's personnel, how staff are motivated to do superior work, the quality of the firm's technology, and the depth of its infrastructure. The main goals of such analysis are two-fold: (1) to identify any latent business risk that may impair the ability of the fund of funds to deliver the desired results, and (2) to identify what, if any, competitive advantage the firm has versus its peers.

BACKGROUND INFORMATION

STAFF INFORMATION

The following series of questions from the AIMA fund of funds questionnaire seeks to ascertain the quantity and quality of personnel as well as who the key decision makers are and how they are compensated. A fund of funds firm's personnel can be its biggest asset. Much of the hedge fund business is relationship-based, so retaining high quality, experienced personnel can be a key competitive advantage versus the competition.

How many employees does the firm currently have?
The number of employees at a fund of funds may correlate to the depth of resources devoted to its work, but it is not indicative of the quality of its personnel and their roles within the firm. A firm with twenty employees, twelve of whom are investment professionals, has a different makeup than a firm with twenty employees, five of whom are investment professionals. In addition, a larger firm with high turnover and more, but less experienced, staff may be less able than a firm with a smaller but more seasoned team. Thus, the question needs to be looked at in conjunction with other questions on staffing.

Show the number of employees by working area.
This amounts to requesting an organizational chart. The level of personnel in each working area is an indication of the resources allocated to that function. Everything else being equal, investors should like to see more resources dedicated to achieving investment performance. A firm that is top-heavy on marketing and client

service personnel and light on research analysts and portfolio managers bears close scrutiny.

What is the greatest and least number of employees the firm has had over the past three years?

This question is intended to establish a recent employment history of the firm and to indicate the stability, or lack thereof, of its personnel. A growing workforce is a sign of a healthy business, while layoffs may signal a more difficult environment. Any significant fluctuation up or down should be investigated further to reveal how these changes may affect the ability of the firm to achieve the investor's investment objectives.

Explain any significant employee turnover.

Some level of employee turnover is to be expected in an asset management business, but an investor will want to understand the circumstances of any important departures and if turnover is likely to recur. The investor will want to understand if turnover was due to upgrading personnel and replacement of less productive employees or whether key personnel have left without comparable or superior replacement. One would expect few unintended employee departures from a successful and growing business that compensates its employees competitively. [Note: Often people appear to leave by their own accord when that is actually the intention of the firm. Firms normally allow "fired" employees to "leave to pursue better opportunities."]

Provide a brief background of key personnel (education, professional background).

Investors should seek to understand how the key decision makers at the firm came to be in the positions they are in. Study the career path of key decision makers, their relevant experience and qualifications, and what may give them a competitive advantage. Investors will want to determine whether expertise was developed in-house or at another company. Look for evidence of continuity, that is, whether key personnel have held jobs for extended periods of time or whether they are likely to jump ship if another opportunity presents itself. Also, a staff that has a variety of skill sets and practical money management experience is generally a favorable sign.

Explain the compensation scheme for key people.
Investors will want to understand how key decision makers are compensated and whether they are given financial incentives to do a superior job. Employees with attractive compensation packages are less likely to leave the firm and more likely to work hard at improving the business.

COMPANY STRUCTURE

The next two questions seek to obtain further information regarding the history, ownership structure, and legal structure of the firm. Business models change over time, and it is important to understand what the current model is, whether it makes sense, and how it relates to past iterations. The goal is get a clear picture of the business as an enterprise, and how it will succeed or not succeed in the future.

Provide details about the firm's current ownership structure and any changes during the past three years.
This question seeks to determine who has, and has had, real financial control over the company. Investors should try to understand where the controlling interests reside, what the incentives of those interests are, and if they coincide with the investor's goal of achieving particular performance objectives.

Provide a short history of the company with the most important milestones.
This question should elicit a picture of where the company has been and where it is headed. Determine what goals have been set and whether they have been achieved. Look for what the business model has been and how it relates to the current state of the company. Identify events in the history of the firm that might indicate

business risks. Ultimately, the investor will want to understand if the firm's history prepares it to deliver the desired investment objectives.

ASSET MANAGEMENT ACTIVITIES

This set of questions seeks to determine the different lines of business the firm engages in, the relative importance of these lines of business, the nature and stability of its respective clients, and the revenues generated by each of the businesses. By sketching out a picture of a firm's current and historical revenue base an investor can make an overall assessment of the health of the business, whether it is allocating resources efficiently, and whether the business is a viable one.

Does the firm conduct any business other than asset management in alternative investments? If so, what is the nature of those other businesses?

This question seeks a disclosure of the true scope of the businesses of the company. Such information is important to know when evaluating and comparing the infrastructure of different funds of funds. Look for cases in which resources are being allocated among various businesses. For example, if the firm is marketing hedge fund managers and that is the prime source of revenue, then the driving focus of the business may not be on fund of funds asset management, but rather selling individual managers. All other things equal, a firm that is focused on fund of funds management should be preferred to one with multiple business lines.

Does the firm also manage investments of other asset classes (including traditional assets)? If so, explain:

Many traditional advisers and money managers have started fund of funds operations. When evaluating a fund of funds, it is important to determine what percentage of time and effort and resources are allocated to the fund of funds business versus other asset management businesses or other lines of business. For example, two fund of funds companies may both have ten investment professionals, but for comparison purposes, it is necessary to know how the resources are allocated. A simple head count may not suffice, regardless of the quality of the individuals. If one firm has only two professionals dedicated to fund of funds management while the other has all ten, the latter firm clearly has committed more personnel to the effort. The key point is to understand the relationship of the different businesses and to what extent the involvement in other businesses will affect the competitive advantage of the firm in the fund of funds arena.

Does the firm manage funds of funds in different strategies? If so, describe.

The scope of fund of funds management operations varies widely. Some run diverse research operations and operate a range of funds of funds. Others may be much more specialized, limiting the scope of investment to a single hedge fund strategy. Managing funds of funds in different strategies requires a broader understanding of strategies and managers. Generally speaking, the broader the scope of the investment mandate, the more resources the fund of funds will need to commit to achieve in-depth coverage of the full range of managers available. Fund of funds managers who offer multiple products will often design them to meet different risk and return objectives. An investor will want to understand how the different products will perform in different market environments. The key point is to understand not only the range of funds of funds offered, but also why they are offered, what hedge fund strategies the fund of funds manager has expertise in, and whether this skill set is optimal to achieve the investor's objectives.

What percentage of assets under management is in funds of funds?

Fund of funds management firms may also consult or provide advisory services to hedge fund investors or other funds of funds. Assets may be under single managers or simply in a general advisory capacity. Although these may be included in assets under management, they are not invested in funds of funds managed by the firm. For analysis and comparison purposes, as well as having a better understanding of the business scope of the company, the investor should examine the breakdown of the assets. For example, a fund of funds with $500 million under management may have $100 million in funds of funds that it manages, $100 million with a single manager in which ten of the fund of funds clients have invested, and $300 million in advisory assets, whereby clients get advice on hedge funds but do not give the firm final discretion over the allocation of assets. Also, in assessing the fund of funds portfolio management abilities of a firm, it is important to understand what percentage of assets are actually in funds of funds versus assets placed with managers or assets that are in traditional portfolios. It is useful to look at the firm as one would look at any other company, estimating revenues from different business lines and costs of operation. Naturally, an investor will want to select a fund of funds that is running a sound business that generates a level of cash flow in excess of its costs of operation.

Which investor group does the firm primarily target?

Many funds of funds management companies create investment products and services that target a specific type of investor. For example, some will focus on the U.S. taxable high-net-worth market. Others may provide products to tax-exempt foundations and endowments. They will design products that specifically cater to the objectives and parameters of the investor group. Investors will generally want to invest alongside other like-minded investors to be sure that the fund of funds manager shares their investment goals. For example, a fund of funds designed for university endowments may have a longer investment horizon than a fund of funds designed for the retail market. The concept extends beyond asset management activities to communication and servicing. The key point is to identify a fund of funds for which you are the target investor to ensure that the investment goals of the investor and fund of funds manager remain aligned.

Provide a list of main clients (including size of assets, duration of client relationship):

Identifying details about the main clients helps provide verification of the experience and expertise of the fund of funds manager. A significant investment from sophisticated investors over extended periods of time can serve as a good reference for a fund of funds. While it is not a substitute for your own due diligence, the fact that an experienced investor has subjected the firm to scrutiny and gone ahead with an investment often serves as a stamp of approval for one's own selection process. Investors will also want to understand the concentration of the fund of funds investor base. If a single investor represents 50 percent of the asset base, this one investor could cause significant disruption to the fund of funds profitability and operational viability if deciding to redeem in full. This question also helps an investor understand the type of business that the asset management company is involved with, the type of relationships that it has, and whether it is in the business of servicing a few large clients as an institutional specialist, a mix of clients as a generalist, or a large number of small investors in a retail operation.

Provide three client references.

It is always valuable to talk to other investors about why they invested and what their experience and level of satisfaction has been. A variation of this question is to ask to talk with ex-clients as well as existing ones. This opportunity allows a potential investor to explore the reasons for a client's leaving and how the separation was handled. Although client references normally involve clients that have been selected by the asset management company, it is still valuable to hear what they have to say about their experiences as an investor. It is expected that references will be positive, but an investor should inquire about the existence of any conflicts of interest. Of course, it is a major warning sign if the client references put forth cannot provide positive feedback and confidence in the quality of the fund of funds manager.

What are the current assets under management (total, traditional, alternative)?

The summary provided here should match the numbers and explanation of the above questions. If they do not, then further discussions with the fund of funds manager are in order to clarify any discrepancies. This question is often asked in a more detailed breakdown covering, for example, such subsets as funds of funds assets, discretionary assets, and advising assets. Again, an investor should evaluate the firm as one would look at any other company, estimating revenues from different business lines and costs of operating. An investor will want to select a fund of funds that is running a sound business that generates a level of cash flow in excess of its costs of operation.

Show the growth of assets under management over the past five years (total, traditional, alternative).

Steady growth in assets indicates a firm that has successfully implemented a business plan. Any large outflows or reduction in assets require further investigation and explanation. A decline in assets can disrupt the operation of a firm by altering the stream of revenues. Similarly, an investor will want to understand the impact of any large inflows on the operation of the business. For example, the performance record of a fund of funds that has had a material level of assets and a consistent infrastructure is more indicative of future prospects than a firm recently staffed around a performance record generated on a small amount of assets. An investor should also consider the asset growth of each fund of funds product managed. In order to sustain a competitive advantage, a fund of funds will need to grow assets to a level sufficient to support the necessary resources.

Show a breakdown of assets under management by client group and by strategy.

Fund of funds operations will be tailored by necessity to focus resources on serving the needs of its main client base or bases. An indication of where this expertise lies can be determined based on the main types of clients. For example, a firm that services predominantly tax-exempt investors may have less familiarity with the needs of a U.S. taxable investor than a firm that services primarily wealthy individuals. Similarly, funds of funds will focus investment resources in the strategy areas where most of their clients' assets are managed. This question should be expanded to include allocation to specific hedge fund strategies, which will clearly indicate the focus of the fund of funds' strategy and expertise. For example, a fund of funds that manages assets primarily invested in Distressed Securities and Event Driven strategies may not have the same level of experience in or research resources dedicated to other strategies, such as Fixed Income Arbitrage or global Macro, as a fund of funds with significant assets invested in diversified programs. A breakdown of assets by client groups and strategy again highlights the kinds of clients that the fund of funds company deals with as well as the investment strategies in which it has experience and expertise.

What is the greatest percentage of assets under management represented by any single and by the three largest clients?
This question focuses on the concentration of the firm's client base and the stability of its revenue. It is important to invest in a fund of funds that is stable and has a management company with sufficient income to support its infrastructure. A sizeable withdrawal of assets from a fund of funds will affect the other investors in the fund and may detrimentally affect the fund of funds, depending on the size of the withdrawal and how it is structured. In a situation in which the bulk of a fund of funds' assets are from one investor, a complete withdrawal of that investor's assets might require the fund of funds to deviate from its manager and strategy diversification objectives because it no longer has the assets to maintain investments in its current mix of hedge funds. In a worst-case scenario, it would affect the fund of funds' survival. In addition, a large investor may influence how the fund of funds is managed. Because that investor's withdrawal might damage or prevent the fund of funds' continued operation, the fund of funds manager may have a conflict of interest between doing what he believes is best for all of the investors

and meeting the demands of one large client. Another example would be when a fund of funds is managing a liquidity differential between what it provides to its investors and what is available from the underlying hedge funds. If a significant liquidity event were to occur, redemption rights for all fund of funds investors might be suspended.

PRODUCT INFORMATION

This series of questions fleshes out and confirms data that can be obtained through database screens. The information gleaned should allow the investor to determine whether the fund is appropriate for investment, from the standpoint of both objectives and parameters. The goal of these questions is to identify a fund that has the highest probability of achieving the investor's goals.

Provide a short description of all products (public and private, where disclosure is possible) of the firm, e.g., funds of funds, advisory mandates, client portfolios, structured products, and so on.
Funds of funds can offer a variety of products and services. While some may manage a single fund of funds, others may manage multiple funds of funds, customized portfolios, and private label funds of funds. They might also provide advisory or consulting services. Products offered may also be available through structured products such as principle protected (guaranteed) funds, linked notes, and options. Having a description of these products and services provides a view of the options and range of expertise available from each fund of funds manager.
   Include at least the following information:
   ■ *Investment objective (including target return and target risk).* A primary goal of the selection process is to identify funds of funds that satisfy the investor's investment objectives, so the information provided in response to this question should be detailed and evaluated carefully. Funds of funds at this level of consideration should generally satisfy threshold objective

requirements based on prior screens. However, a more detailed confirmation of these goals both in the initial product identified as well as in other products managed by the firm should be achieved at this stage.

■ *Target investors.* Funds of funds are normally designed with a specific target investor group in mind, with features targeted to the needs of that particular audience. The threshold investor-type questions, such as taxable or non-taxable, U.S. versus non-U.S., should have been screened for by this stage. Confirm them in detail and ask for more specifics explaining how the product is suitable for its target investor group.

■ *Legal structure.* As discussed previously, funds of funds can be offered in a number of different forms such as limited partnerships, limited liability companies, unit trusts, registered investment companies, mutual funds, and SICAVs (the acronym for Societe d'Investissement a Capital Variable, a form of unit trust or mutual fund registered in France, Belgium, or Luxembourg). They may be organized in the United States, in tax havens such as Bermuda or the Cayman Islands, or in any country offering investment fund structure. The legal structure may be important for a variety of reasons. Tax treatment of gains and losses, as well as the impact of any local tax scheme, is a significant consideration, as such matters will vary depending upon structure and tax election. The legal infrastructure and investor rights are subject to protection afforded by a court system and the integrity of the law. Also, for some entities restrictions may prevent investing in certain types of structures (such as private limited partnerships) or in certain jurisdictions (such as outside the United States).

■ *Asset allocation.* Funds of funds with similar descriptions and investment objectives will often have very different combinations of strategies. They will also vary widely in how strategies are weighted and the number of hedge funds they incorporate to gain the strategy exposures. Strategies excluded by an investor's parameter should be screened prior to this stage. It is also advisable to confirm parameter compliance at this level. Asset allocation is a good aid for categorizing funds and for reviewing their performance. It also provides a means with which a potential investor can track how the fund of funds composition has varied and is likely to vary over time.

■ *Number of funds in the portfolio.* A major benefit of investing in a fund of funds is diversification. The number of funds that are invested in varies widely among funds of funds. It may range from two or three funds to over one hundred. Most appear to fall in the fifteen- to thirty-fund range. Check whether the number of funds is mandated by plan or if it varies over time. The number of funds as a measure of diversification offered is another good categorization factor.

■ *Current size.* A snapshot of fund assets is an important categorization factor and may be a parameter issue as well, as some investors limit the percentage of the fund of funds that their assets can represent. The number of investors is also a factor to consider. Further, also look at the fund of funds' asset growth over time in order to evaluate the volatility of assets as well as to determine a base for performance review.

■ *Date of inception.* Funds of funds that begin investing after the date specified (which allows time for an adequate track record) can be screened. Confirm the date for the selected product and others offered at this stage. Because back tests and pro forma performance records are often used in the industry, the date of inception should be checked against the performance record dates to determine when actual returns began.

■ *Fee structure.* Fund of funds fees can vary widely. They usually consist of an annual management fee paid monthly or quarterly as a percentage of assets invested in the fund of funds. They may also include an incentive fee, which is a percentage of profits, sometimes above a minimum return hurdle, usually paid quarterly or annually. Fee structures are often cited as "one and ten," which means a 1 percent management fee and a 10 percent incentive fee. (See Chapter 4 for a detailed discussion on fees.)

▪ *Conditions for subscriptions and redemptions.* The subscription process describes how to invest in a fund of funds. The redemption process describes how to get your money out of a fund of funds. These processes will vary among funds of funds as to timing, amounts, notices, and fees. Look for lead times, notice periods for entering and exiting the fund, payout timing, holdbacks, and other features. (See Chapter 4 for a more detailed discussion.)

▪ *State any other costs and fees borne by the product in addition to the fees mentioned above.* Funds of funds normally pay routine accounting, legal, and administrative fees. Start-up costs, marketing fees, and other costs may also be charged to the fund of funds. The performance of a fund of funds will equal the collective returns of the underlying hedge funds less the fee and expense cost burden of the fund of funds. Therefore, it is important to have a clear picture of what this total amount is when comparing funds of funds, as it directly impacts the net returns to the investor. Also determine whether all fees stated are also reflected in the published performance record.

▪ *Describe the minimum investment amounts of the different types of products and services.* Fund of funds minimum investment requirements may range from thousands of dollars for registered investment products to millions of dollars. As a parameter, minimum investments should be screened prior to this level and confirmed during due diligence. But even when the stated minimum is above the target level, it doesn't hurt to contact the fund of funds manager to determine whether there is any flexibility on minimum investment size.

▪ *Does the firm specialize in any product or group of products? If so, please explain.* Some funds of funds specialize in certain products, such as single strategy funds, or funds targeted at specific investor groups. This can be a significant inclusion or exclusion factor, depending on the needs of the investor. When the search objective includes a single strategy mandate, for example, the single strategy specialist may be the perfect solution. If the objective is to select a diversified market neutral fund, the single strategy specialist would not be a stand-alone fit.

PERFORMANCE

Most performance data are available through performance databases, but investors should obtain performance documentation for the products being evaluated along with an explanation of what the performance represents. Performance can be quoted either net of fees, gross of fees, or may represent a pro forma back test of current allocations. By obtaining standardized performance for the various funds under consideration an investor can make summary quantitative comparisons across funds. Although these statistical screens serve as an indication, investors need to look beyond the raw performance to what the underlying exposures that produced that performance were. All performance data need to be related back to the investment process that produced those returns. This process is covered in more detail in Chapter 9, but it is worth emphasizing at this point that while historical performance is not necessarily indicative of future performance, its evaluation in the context of the qualitative environment at the time compared to the present will provide insight for expectations going forward.

Provide historical performance data for all products (in electronic form, when possible), including monthly returns, standard deviation (annualized), three largest drawdowns and recovery periods, and percentage of positive and negative months.
Fund of funds performance data are usually provided net of fees, but confirm this for all numbers provided. Numbers should be provided as monthly percentage increases or decreases (January: +2 percent, February: -1.5 percent). Having information provided electronically allows the data to be analyzed and compared more easily using spreadsheets or analytical software. A variety of statistics looking at measures of return and volatility are often used. It is better to calculate these statistics for each fund rather than rely on

the calculations provided by the fund of funds, in order to ensure a consistent methodology across all funds of funds under evaluation. Standard deviation is a measure of volatility that is often used as an indication of risk. A drawdown is the peak to valley measure of loss. A drawdown period ends when a new high is established. The recovery period measures the number of months it takes to achieve a new high once a drawdown occurs. A drawdown is measured as a percentage loss, such as a 10 percent drawdown. The percentage of positive months and negative months is a measure of consistency. The higher the percentage of positive months, the more consistent is the performance. It is calculated by taking the total number of positive months and dividing it by the total number of months considered. For example, if the total number of months considered is one hundred, and eighty were positive and twenty were negative, the percentage of positive months would be 80 percent (80/100) and the percentage of negative months would be 20 percent (20/100).

State in which period performance is actual or pro forma (i.e., backtracked).
Some funds of funds may report pro forma or other types of performance, such as private accounts, associated with other vehicles in reported track records. To get a clear understanding of past performance, as well as using a level playing field for comparing funds of funds performance, it is necessary to understand the source for all performance information.

Is performance net of fees to the investor?
Funds of funds fees are almost always reported "net of fees." Although gross numbers may be valuable when the fee overhead may have been reduced or changed, the net performance is usually the best representation of the historical performance achieved by investors and also the accurate way to compare one fund of funds to another.

SUMMARY

The fund of funds responses to the questions discussed in this chapter will provide investors with a good base of understanding of the firm's business history, infrastructure, operations, investor base, performance record, and associated strengths/weaknesses in these areas. From this overview, the next step is to investigate in detail the core portfolio management activities of the fund of funds.

Issues in Due Diligence: Portfolio Management

9

F UNDS OF FUNDS seek to generate returns above that of the overall hedge fund industry by opportunistically selecting hedge fund strategies, substrategies, and managers, and weighting them differently than the overall industry allocates assets to them. Fund of fund performance is produced by the underlying strategy exposures and by whatever excess return, or "alpha," a hedge fund manager operating within a strategy can produce. As with investors in traditional investment classes such as stocks and bonds, not every hedge fund investor can outperform the industry, because collectively all the participants constitute the industry. A fund of funds manager, therefore, must be more skilled than his competitors in strategy allocation and manager selection in order to produce superior returns over time.

The questions in this chapter are from the Alternative Investment Management Association (AIMA) Illustrative Questionnaire for Due Diligence of Fund of Fund Managers (see Appendix A) and address how a fund of funds goes about selecting strategies and managers and building its portfolio. They in total attempt to illuminate a fund of funds' investment process and what investment edge a fund of funds may possess. Understanding the investment process allows the investor to formulate rational return expectations for the future and determine whether those expectations are in line with the investor's goals.

ASSET ALLOCATION/STYLE SELECTION

The set of questions that follows is designed to help the investor understand how asset allocation decisions at the strategy level are made by a fund of funds. The investor will want to understand the methodology and frequency of asset allocation shifts, as well as who is involved. Understanding a fund of funds' decision-making process allows an investor to assess prospective strategy allocations and whether the fund of funds has an edge in this area. Questions regarding the interaction of macro-level strategy allocation decisions and decisions regarding individual managers will be addressed in the portfolio construction section.

What is the firm's asset allocation process?
The selection, combination, and weighting of hedge funds in a portfolio is the core of a fund of funds' asset management operation. The asset allocation process begins with an investment philosophy and a view of what drives the performance in hedge fund strategies. For example, one fund of funds manager might see the hedge fund industry as a maze where the key to success is identifying the best managers and combining them in a fund of funds. Another fund of funds manager might see the hedge fund universe as a combination of strategies that will be in and out of favor, depending on market cycles. Their approach is to identify the "in favor" strategies and allocate to the "best" managers within those strategies. The former approach puts a higher premium on manager selection and the latter places more importance on style selection. The selection of a hedge fund manager, however, is in large part a substrategy selection. In addition, all fund of funds managers, either purposefully or unknowingly, express a macro outlook for markets in the combination of managers in their funds of funds.

When aggregated, the collective exposures of the underlying hedge fund managers will be more vulnerable to certain market-related factors and less to others. For example, if the exposures of a fund of funds specializing in equity hedge strategies are aggregated, it might be found that the fund of funds is 50 percent net long small-cap U.S. value stocks. Aside from the distinct approaches of the various hedge funds, the fund of funds has a large small-cap value stock bet on; it is positioned to make money in a rising U.S. small-cap value environment and to lose money if small-cap value stocks fall. This macro exposure may reflect the view of the fund of funds manager at the time, be an artifact of the manager selection process, or be a result of a stated selection bias, such as being invested in U.S. equity hedge funds that will always be at least 60 percent net long.

On what basis does the firm define and change the asset allocation of the portfolios?

Funds of funds will often use very general language in their offering memorandums in describing their asset allocation process, so it is important to understand this process in more detail. Usually, the asset allocation process can be described in terms of included or eligible strategies and strategy concentration. The types of strategies might be listed, such as Merger Arbitrage, Convertible Arbitrage, and Relative Value Arbitrage, or generally described, such as "long bias equity strategies." Strategy concentrations are usually stated as a maximum exposure, such as "no more than 20 percent in any strategy." Funds of funds may also state minimum levels of strategy diversification. Be aware, however, that hedge fund strategy definitions are not standardized, so make sure to understand how the fund of funds manager defines the strategies it uses. These definitions might be rigidly set and require notice to investors prior to changing, or may be loose definitions that can vary from time to time at the discretion of the fund of funds manager. Determine which policy the fund of funds follows.

On what periodicity is the asset allocation of the portfolio reviewed?

Funds of funds may review asset allocation on a monthly or quarterly basis, as was noted in Chapter 8, although some managers will conduct a less-frequent evaluation. In understanding how static or nimble a fund of funds operation is in rebalancing and changing allocations, keep in mind a couple of things. First, because there is a time, and, in some cases, a transaction cost impact to redeeming from a portfolio and reallocating, a fund of funds that is not growing or adding significant assets has a different asset allocation process than a fund of funds where assets are coming in on a monthly basis. Static assets may require quarterly or annual liquidity with a notice period. If that is the case, then a decision made in May often may not be implemented until November.

How does that work? As discussed earlier, if the underlying funds to be redeemed require a 45-day notice period to the end of the quarter, then a late May notice would miss the June redemption period, so it would not be effective until October 1. In those cases, the assets are not immediately available, but usually the majority of the assets would be available for the following month. The first reallocation after the redemption decision made in May, then, would occur in November. On the other hand, for assets coming in, the decision made at the end of May could result in an allocation on June 1.

The allocation philosophy should match the frequency of reallocation. A fund of funds that makes allocation decisions on an annual basis should be making decisions based on long-term shifts in financial markets. A fund of funds that has the ability to make more frequent adjustments may be able to react to or anticipate shorter-term trends such as fund flows. In addition to understanding the asset allocation process, investors will want to understand, and where possible to quantify, the value added by the process.

For nonstandard products, to what extent can the investor be involved in the asset allocation process?

This question refers to customized funds of funds or hedge fund baskets. Many fund of funds managers will construct customized funds of funds. Some will also allow investor input in the asset allocation process. And, an even smaller number actually support active portfolio management by the client. In addition to offering "off the shelf" funds of funds, some management companies will work with a client to design and build customized fund of funds portfolios as well as private label funds of funds for distribution. In these instances, the investor should be able to participate in the design and ongoing management. This may take the form of setting the objectives and parameters for the fund of funds, as well as being involved in portfolio management and the ongoing decision-making process, including approval of managers to be included in the custom fund.

The concept of discretion is important here. Discretion indicates who is responsible for the investment decisions. For a typical customized fund of funds, the fund of funds manager has investment discretion and the client sets the investment guidelines. The fund of funds manager still retains discretion over the investment decisions. In some cases, the investor will form an investment committee with representation from both the fund of funds manager and the investor. An arrangement whereby the investor has full discretion over the fund and the fund of funds manager simply provides advice is in essence an advisory or consultative one.

Do investment guidelines exist for all products? If so, please provide a sample.

Almost all funds of funds have some type of investment guidelines that describe how the fund will invest. They may identify types of strategies, instruments, geographic regions, concentration, or leverage. They will vary widely in description and in the level of detail and constraint that is "hard wired" into the investment process. The investment guidelines provide the investor much better insight into the actual investment approach, and a more precise basis for categorization and comparisons than general fund of funds descriptions such as "absolute return" or "market neutral."

How can the guidelines be altered?

The guidelines are the fund of funds' rules for investing. However, rules that can be changed at any time or in an arbitrary manner are of little value for investor reliance, so it is important to get a clear understanding of how and if they can be changed. Common methods might be by the consent of a majority of investors or by providing all investors timely notice of guideline changes, thereby allowing them time to redeem their investment if the amended guidelines no longer meet their investment objectives and parameters.

DUE DILIGENCE CRITERIA IN MANAGER SELECTION

A fund of funds relies on its underlying hedge fund managers to produce performance, and thus the manager selection process is paramount to fund of funds performance. By selecting managers who have an edge over their peers, a fund of funds can produce excess returns. Prior to allocating to a hedge fund (or hiring a hedge fund manager to trade a separate account), the fund of funds manager conducts an investigation to determine the suitability of the investment. An investor will want to understand what criteria a fund of funds manager uses to identify and select managers, who are the key decision makers, what is their level of expertise, and what resources are devoted to the effort.

On what principles are the firm's due diligence process based?

Funds of funds take varied approaches to due diligence on hedge fund managers. Some rely heavily on the representations of the hedge funds and general measures such as assets managed and industry reputation, while others put more effort into independently verifying the information provided by hedge funds. The due diligence process is inseparable from the investment process, and ongoing investment decisions are dependent on the insights provided by ongoing due diligence efforts. A fund of funds' philosophy and due diligence framework, including how it handles such issues as risk, potential for return, and oversight of managers are typically included in the firm's description of its principles.

What is the firm's due diligence process? Provide examples of reports and working papers, when available.

The due diligence process can be described as the gathering, verification, and evaluation of all available material information. What is considered to be "available" or "material" will depend on each firm's due diligence principles and overall investment philosophy. Because hedge funds are private, there is no standardized disclosure, and some firms provide less information than others. Also, the level of information required from a manager will vary from one fund of funds to the next. Accordingly, the universe of acceptable hedge funds for each will also differ.

In general, the due diligence process begins with the universe of hedge funds and then screens down to those selected for investment. How a fund of funds gets from a few thousand managers to perhaps twenty involves a series of qualitative and quantitative screens. For example, the initial screen may be based on asset size and length of track record. This might be followed by a performance screen with minimum returns and maximum volatility cutoffs. The next step would be a more detailed evaluation of a short list of hedge funds. In most cases, this more detailed work will result in an investment opinion of some form detailing the reasons to invest or not invest with a manager. When possible, examine the outputs from the due diligence process in detail to better understand how the fund of funds goes about identifying hedge fund managers who have an edge.

What is the minimum required essential criteria a manager has to meet, if any, to pass the due diligence?

The most common minimum requirements are easily quantified indications of experience and size of operation, such as length of track record or assets managed. By way of example, a fund of funds that requires that a hedge fund manager have a three-year track record and $300 million under management is looking to invest with more mature managers. Alternatively, minimum requirements could be informational. In general, minimum requirements can be in the form of: (1) scope of information,

(2) amount of detail, (3) frequency, (4) time lines, (5) veracity. For example, consider the progressive degrees of information that could be required by a fund of funds manager before it invests with a hedge fund.

Explain the portfolio holdings as follows:

a. In a summary	**b.** At position-level detail
a. Quarterly	**b.** Daily
a. With a one-month lag	**b.** The next day
a. Relying on the manager reports	**b.** From an independent third-party source

Although both the a's and b's require an evaluation of a hedge fund portfolio, the minimum requirements differ significantly.

Do you conduct on-site visits with the managers?

The best (or perhaps worst) story involving site verification is one of a hedge fund manager whose stated office address turned out to be that of a hot-dog stand. Besides confirming the existence of an actual money management operation, on-site visits are important to facilitate face-to-face meetings with the various firm members to hear their description of their activities and function, view them in their work environment, see their processes and systems demonstrated, and be able to ask questions.

How much time is spent with each manager during the due diligence process, both before initial investment and each year thereafter?

Understanding the amount of time spent with a manager or the number of times a fund of funds manager meets with underlying managers is a starting point in assessing how thoroughly a fund of funds manager knows a hedge fund before investing. However, the quality and context of the time spent is even more telling. For example, time spent with the portfolio manager discussing positions, market views, portfolio construction, and risk controls is more valuable than meeting with the director of marketing. Some funds of funds will quantify this process in the number of visits to a manager prior to investing and visits per year once an investment is made. The goal is to determine that the fund of funds maintains an effective initial and ongoing review process in order to remain on top of portfolio exposures and detect early warning signals from managers encountering problems.

How many new managers do you analyze per year? In how many of the analyzed managers do you finally invest?

Some good general statistics can be derived from these numbers, particularly when taken in conjunction with the resources dedicated to the effort. For example, it is more likely that a more thorough job will be done with eight professionals evaluating one hundred managers a year as compared to two professionals trying to accomplish the same task. Also, because due diligence is ongoing, significant resources are required to competently search for new talent and also stay abreast of current investments. Look for and compare the overall scope of the due diligence effort, the detail and frequency of review, the level of manager coverage, and the resources applied to accomplish these tasks. It takes time to build a familiarity with managers and their strategies, so experienced personnel with a track record of analyzing managers are important.

Do you carry out due diligence checks on the target investee funds' administrator or any other service provider? If so, please describe.

The hedge fund administrators and other service providers such as auditors, attorneys, and bankers are critical to the successful functioning of the hedge fund. Just as the fund of funds will be dependent upon the underlying hedge fund for performance, it also will be dependent on that hedge fund's service providers. A fund of funds manager should know who they are and that they are professionally qualified and reputable. Also, a fund of funds should provide verification that a relationship does indeed exist.

How many managers are currently on your approved list?
Fund of funds managers will, of course, have a list of the managers in which they invest. In addition, they will also have a larger set of funds that are approved for investment, but currently have not received any assets from the fund of funds. Generally, for managers on the larger approved list, due diligence is close to completion or investment is subject to final due diligence. Think of this as an assessment of bench strength. The due diligence process takes time to complete properly. In order to maintain investment capacity and flexibility, a fund of funds should have a source of investment opportunities readily available. Look for manager depth in a strategy as well as diversified strategy coverage (at least within the mandate of the fund of funds), even in those strategies in which the fund is not currently invested.

How much capacity is available from managers on the approved list? Please provide breakdown by strategy.
Hedge funds periodically close to new investments. If a fund of funds no longer has access to a core manager, then the composition of its portfolio will change going forward. Depending on a fund of funds' relationship with the underlying hedge funds, it may retain some level of capacity for its fund of funds. For example, if a hedge fund on the approved list has remaining capacity of $200 million, the fund of funds manager may make arrangements with the hedge fund to retain $50 million for a period of time for its fund of funds. If a firm runs multiple funds of funds and/or private portfolios, it is also valuable to understand how the limited capacity of a particular hedge fund will be allocated among the various entities to ensure that one product or client is not favored over another.

PORTFOLIO CONSTRUCTION

This series of questions should help the investor understand how the asset allocation and manager selection functions are combined in the construction of the ultimate fund of funds portfolio. Find out how and why underlying hedge fund managers are hired and fired, what kind of exposures the portfolio construction process has led to in the past, and what kind of exposures it is likely to produce in the future. These expectations should then be measured against the investor objectives.

What are the qualitative and quantitative criteria used in your portfolio construction process?

While perhaps every fund of funds uses some blend of qualitative and quantitative inputs, the manner and weight given to each will vary drastically from fund of funds to fund of funds. For example, some take a highly quantitative approach, analyzing hedge fund return streams for correlation to various markets and other hedge funds, stress testing various combinations of strategies and funds to determine the potential impact of significant market shifts, and looking to determine, based on historical performance data, the optimal portfolio of hedge funds necessary to achieve the goals of the fund of funds. Critics say that this approach is flawed due to a lack of data and lack of consistency within the existing data. This results from the short history of most hedge funds; a large number of funds have been in existence for less than five years. Because of this, few, if any, have experienced full market cycles and the variety of market conditions necessary to give this approach a high degree of predictive value.

Also, most hedge funds have changed over time in terms of asset size, investment approach, and even decision makers. In addition, hedge funds have many more moving parts in terms of the financial instruments and exposures in their portfolios. Because of this variability, the performance produced during a certain type of market condition may not be indicative of how they might perform the next time a similar market event occurs. For example, the historical performance of a large-cap value mutual fund in a falling stock market might indicate what kind of performance to expect the next time the market declines. But a hedge fund that lost money in a declining market might begin buying put options on an ongoing basis to hedge its long stock exposures. The next time the market declines, it does not lose money, and may even generate a profit. The quantitative analysis would not predict this outcome, incorporating instead incorrect expectations into the portfolio construction.

At the other end of the spectrum are funds of funds that rely almost entirely on qualitative inputs. They may place significant emphasis on a manager's background, experience, and professional reputation. The focus is on identifying the best manager, although that label is undefined. Critics point out that the best managers change over time and in a number of instances have ended their stardom with substantial losses. In some cases, the "best" were merely on the edge of their strategies in terms of risk, or were involved in falsified pricing or even investing in a manner other than what they represented to investors. Most funds of funds actually construct their portfolios with a combination of both quantitative and qualitative inputs, often taking the form of a quantitative framework with qualitative fine-tuning.

What is the average turnover of managers within the portfolios?

Over the life of a fund of funds, the portfolio of hedge funds the fund of funds manager invests in will change. Manager turnover is usually described in terms of the number of managers dropped or fired in a single year or per year over time. It is important to understand the relationship between turnover and the historical performance of the fund of funds. An investor will want to know to what extent the track record was produced by current underlying managers. Funds of funds will hire and fire managers for a variety of reasons. The main reasons are

1 lack of, or bad, performance
2 due diligence issues
3 strategy allocation change (by fund of funds)
4 manager goes out of business (which is really a consequence *to* the fund of funds rather than an action taken *by* the fund of funds manager).

Considered in isolation, the degree of turnover may not indicate much. A fund of funds with high manager turnover in a particular year might have a problem with lapses in due diligence, or it may have shifted its macro outlook and, accordingly, changed its strategy allocation by moving out of some managers and into others. A fund of funds with low turnover may be paying little attention to its portfolio, or after careful review may be content with the performance of its managers. To make the turnover number meaningful, investors must put it in the context of the fund of funds portfolio management approach, performance, and the comparative turnover of other funds of funds. Note that changes in market cycles result in shifts in the relative opportunities of the various hedge fund strategies. In such periods, expect to see more aggressive shifting in fund of funds portfolios, and therefore expect to see increased manager turnover as funds of funds make adjustments.

Does the turnover of managers in different portfolios vary substantially?

A fund of funds manager may operate a variety of funds or multiple manager portfolios. Differences in the turnover among these portfolios may indicate a specific problem, inconsistent management approach, or differing realignments based on distinct portfolio objectives and composition. A manager unsuitable for one portfolio as a result of due diligence issues is thus unsuitable and should be removed from all. But when different funds of funds pursue different goals, or when they allocate based on a different macro view, a hedge fund removed from one portfolio may remain or be added to another. The question should be raised, and the answer should fit into and be explained by the fund of funds portfolio construction process.

What are the main reasons for managers to be excluded from an existing portfolio?

The reasons for exclusion will normally be tied to a step in the selection process. They may have been screened out due to parameter constraints such as minimum assets under management or length of track record. They may be excluded due to substandard performance relative to their peers. At the next stage, they may be excluded because they failed to satisfy the due diligence process. If they have made it past the due diligence screen, they might still be excluded because their strategy does not fit the objectives of the fund of funds, or perhaps the strategy fits, but another manager is deemed to be a better choice.

Has a manager included in a portfolio of the firm ever gone out of business due to losses? If yes, what are the lessons learned from that experience, and how have they been applied to the ongoing operation?

Hedge fund managers expect to generate the majority of their compensation through the 20 percent profit participation. In addition, most have a high-water mark, which means they need to generate profits above the previous highest level of an investor's money before earning fees. When a hedge fund has large losses, the prospect of recouping the losses and getting into profit participation territory again is remote for the existing assets. Because of the losses, it is also difficult to raise new investment capital. In addition, the hedge fund may also be faced with redemptions of existing investor assets.

In these situations, a hedge fund may be forced to shut down its fund because it cannot operate on reduced assets that are currently paying only a management fee with no near-term hope for earning an incentive fee. For example, consider a hedge fund with $300 million in assets. It earns a $3 million management fee, and if it generates a 10 percent profit, it will earn a $6 million incentive fee. However, if this fund suffers a 40 percent loss, it will drop to an asset level of $180 million. It will now earn a $1.8 million management fee and will have to generate better than a 67 percent return before earning any incentive on existing money. Even if the fund's operations are covered by the $1.8 million, the manager and key people in the firm may not feel that there is enough of an incentive to continue. This happens at a higher frequency after market transitions. For example, there was an increase in hedge fund closures in 2002 and 2003 following the collapse of the equity markets and the related losses and limited profit outlook for some long-biased equity hedge managers.

In a fund liquidation situation, there are a number of risks to a fund of funds, depending on how deep a market there is for the liquidating fund's holdings. When they are illiquid, there is the risk of additional losses as the remaining investments are marked down and "dumped." There is also a risk that some percentage of the final portfolio cannot be liquidated, resulting in a lockup for a period of time that prevents the fund of funds from redeeming its assets from the fund.

Are portfolios transparent to the investor?

A fund of funds portfolio consists of investments in a number of hedge funds, which in turn are invested in a variety of securities. Although a few funds of funds are transparent down to the security level to their investors, this is far from the industry norm today. Transparency to fund of funds investors means that the hedge funds that the fund of funds is invested with are disclosed, and in some cases a breakdown of their performance is reported as well.

Because the hedge funds selected are the final product of the fund of funds managers' efforts and expertise, funds of funds are reluctant to make that information publicly available and allow others to "piggyback" on their investment ideas or trade against them. Even though some will openly disclose their holdings, most will require some degree of confidentiality from investors. In addition, funds of funds may also ask that the investors agree that they will not invest with any hedge fund manager disclosed by the fund of funds other than through the fund of funds.

The benefit of transparency to investors is a confirmation of the underlying investments and an understanding of performance attribution on a manager-by-manager as well as strategy-by-strategy basis. This provides investors with far better insight into how that money is being managed than a monthly fund of funds composite report.

How does the firm secure capacity with top-class managers now and in the future?

Managers who perform well attract assets and will often reach capacity quickly. Some funds will close to all investments, while others will close to any new investors, but will still accept money from existing investors. Although these managers do not necessarily perform well in the future, funds of funds establish relationships through investment. If the manager becomes selective in accepting new or additional assets, the fund of funds will enjoy the preferential treatment given to early and existing investors. Funds of funds may also seek to retain capacity by contract, often attaching a right to increase its investment by some factor as a condition to making the initial investment.

What is the competitive edge in the firm's investment strategy?

The competitive edge is what will allow the fund of funds manager to deliver returns in excess of similarly situated products. There is no one place to look for a competitive edge. It may be the personnel and experience of the firm. It may be a quantifiable factor such as research access and technology, or something more intangible such as access to the "inside track" at the big Wall Street firms. It may be access to top-performing managers. In any case, a fund of funds manager should be able to make a case that the fund has a competitive edge. Investors will want to make their own appraisal and see if they agree with that assessment.

SUMMARY

The portfolio management activities of a fund of funds are what drives its performance. A fund of funds' ability to meet the performance objectives of its investment products is directly linked to how it categorizes and selects managers its methods of portfolio construction. An investor should be satisfied with the competency of the fund of funds' people, operations, manager selection and portfolio construction processes, and risk management procedures.

Issues in Due Diligence: Risk Management 10

F UND OF FUNDS RISK MANAGEMENT can be separated into two areas: business and investment. The investment risk management can be further divided between portfolio level and fund (or manager) level. The business risks concern the noninvestment risks of the fund of funds, including operations, legal issues, and compliance matters.

In assessing risk management at the investment level, it's understood that some risk must be taken in order to outperform the industry index. By selecting some strategies over others relative to the hedge fund industry as a whole, certain market risks are assumed over others. Manager selection may include the choice of so-called outlier managers who can deliver higher relative returns but also have a risk profile that differs from that of their strategy group in general. The question in all cases is whether the risk taken is merited by the potential rewards. A sound risk management practice will define the realm of possible allocations so that the set of possible results is within an established tolerance range.

When hedge funds are selected for inclusion in a fund of funds portfolio, that selection is based on both an expectation of what the hedge fund manager will do in his portfolio as well as the contribution that the manager's strategy will make to the overall portfolio given the current and forecasted economic environment. Risk management focuses on two questions: (1) Is the individual fund manager maintaining an investment discipline consistent with what was represented to that fund of funds manager? (2) Are the risks and exposures carried by the hedge fund manager still in line with the risk range at the time of allocation, or has the environment shifted so that they now represent a change in the risk-reward characteristics of the strategy? As you can see, it is important to have a solid understanding of the former so that the latter can be properly evaluated. How this is accomplished depends on whether the fund of funds has transparency.

TRANSPARENCY AND SEPARATELY MANAGED ACCOUNTS

TRANSPARENCY

Hedge funds are normally unregulated investment vehicles generally not required to report performance or portfolio holdings on a daily basis. Although managers typically report portfolio performance and, in some cases, holdings information to investors monthly, there is no guarantee that the intramonth trades of a manager follow expectations. This monthly treatment is the standard level of information available to most funds of funds, but a growing number demand a much higher level. In order to ensure daily compliance with investment guidelines, it is necessary to have portfolio-level information on a daily basis. This is accomplished through transparency.

Transparency is a controversial issue in the industry today, both for investors and managers. Smart investors demand it, but some managers are reluctant to provide it. Soros Fund Management is both a hedge fund manager and an investor in other hedge funds.

In talking to their organization a number of years ago on the subject of transparency, this author was told, "Full transparency is an absolute necessity. We would never invest in a hedge fund without it." For investors in his own funds, however, Soros did not allow any transparency.

We often hear the word "transparent" used in relation to investments these days. In *Merriam-Webster's Collegiate Dictionary* "transparency" means: the state of being easily detected, readily understood, and free from pretense or deceit. In the investment world, it is often used to describe the need for more access to information on a timely basis, particularly where there has been a fraud or serious misunderstanding on the part of the investment community as to the true activities, risks, and opportunities of an investment. For the manager of a fund of funds, it is a term used to describe whether the fund of funds has access to the day-to-day position-level exposure information underlying its hedge fund investments.

The hedge fund industry has historically been non-transparent. While the industry was small and primarily consisted of wealthy individuals, this remained the status quo. But the lack of any outside view into the actual goings on of individual funds led to abuse— sometimes introduced intentionally from the beginning, and sometimes occurring as a response to mistakes and market situations that were unforeseen by the hedge fund managers. The lack of transparency in the hedge fund and the fund of funds industry stands as a significant barrier to investment.

In a narrow sense, transparency is essential for a fund of funds to know what it is invested in. It has broader significance in the context of fund of funds risk management activities. Access to the investment portfolio of hedge funds is recent, and the development of the tools and expertise to evaluate the risk exposures and volatility of the various investment styles even more recent. This situation has resulted in a segmented business model, with some funds of funds fully transparent, some partially so, and some not so at all. It is important to understand which approach a fund of funds manager follows.

Non-Transparency. A fund of funds manager who follows a non-transparent philosophy has no direct knowledge of the holdings or investment activities of the underlying hedge funds. Accordingly, the actual risks of the hedge fund portfolio cannot be determined. Many managers have never seen an actual hedge fund portfolio. They derive their understanding of the hedge funds' investment activities and strategies from what they are told by the hedge fund managers. There is very limited risk-monitoring ability and no risk-management ability.

Semi-Transparency. The semi-transparent fund of funds manager gets portfolio level information from the hedge fund manager or its prime broker at the direction of the manager. This provides the fund of funds with portfolio-level risk exposures or, in some cases, position-level detail of the account at the prime broker. However, it does not provide the fund of funds with the whole picture. As the hedge fund manager controls all the information, items such as other accounts, derivatives that are off the balance sheet, and private investments may not be disclosed. There is also the issue of how the instruments are priced by the hedge fund manager. A fund of funds manager may not even know the actual amount of assets that should be in the account. For example, a portfolio feed from the prime broker may show $100 million in investments, but what if the hedge fund has raised $300 million from investors of which $200 million has actually been lost or diverted? The $100 million would have $300 million in investor claims. In this arrangement, the hedge fund manager has control over both the assets and the information relating to their status. Without the hedge fund manager's full, accurate, and timely disclosure, the true state of the investment is impossible to know. Compared to the non-transparent fund of funds, there is an improved level of risk monitoring capability. Risk management tools are limited to redemption, but the higher level of information allows for an earlier notice.

Full, "Closed-System" Transparency. For many investors, allocating to a private hedge fund where trading, pricing, reporting, and custody and control of the asset are in the hands of one company and perhaps one individual is not a prudent way to invest. However, a growing number of funds of funds operate in a fully transparent environment requiring complete information about a hedge fund investment and a separation of custody and control of the investment assets from the manager. Investment into a full, closed-system transparent account allows the fund of funds manager to track the money from initial investment into the fund and subsequent investment into securities. In the closed-system investment structure, no security is allowed to be purchased into or sold out of the account outside of investment guidelines approved by the fund of funds manager. Additionally, all investors in a particular account are known since the structure is set up and traded exclusively for the fund of funds manager. Pricing can be done using independent sources and following a consistent methodology. For the transparent fund of funds, the highest level of risk monitoring can be conducted and real risk management is possible.

MANAGED ACCOUNT STRUCTURES

In order to achieve full "closed-system" transparency, a fund of funds must access a hedge fund manager through a separate account rather than through an investment in its hedge fund. A separate account, also called a "managed account" or "separately managed account," is basically a brokerage account owned, controlled, or overseen by the fund of funds. The hedge fund manager is under contract to trade the account in the same way—pari passu—as the manager's hedge fund is traded.

The separate account provides the fund of funds with a number of benefits over a hedge fund investment. First, the fund of funds has full awareness of, and control over, all aspects of the arrangement, including all asset flows into and out of the account. In addition, daily access to all positions allows the fund of funds to independently price the portfolio, eliminating the risk of manager price manipulations. Furthermore, the separate account also allows for high-level risk monitoring, and the fund of funds can confirm that the manager is adhering to the represented investment style.

One of the greatest benefits is that the separate account allows the fund of funds to take corrective action if a risk violation occurs. Because the account is controlled or overseen by the fund of funds, it can instruct the manager to reduce a position in the event of a risk parameter violation. If a rogue manager refuses, the fund of funds can step in at any time to remove the manager and liquidate the portfolio as necessary.

PRICING RISK CASE STUDY: LIPPER

An example illustrating why it is important for fund of funds managers to ensure the integrity of security prices is the 2002 blowup of hedge funds run by New York–based investment advisory firm Lipper & Co. In November 2001, Lipper, which had two convertible arbitrage funds, sent a letter to investors stating that each of the funds was up approximately 7 percent year-to-date. Then, in February 2002, Lipper stated that the larger of the two funds, Lipper Convertibles L.P., was down approximately 33 percent since the beginning of the year and more than 40 percent since November 2001. According to the *Wall Street Journal*, the reasons for the dramatic devaluation were "the extraordinary combined severity of 2001 events," including the "fallout from the California energy crises, the decline in telecom stocks, the September terrorist attacks, and the market uncertainty amidst the war on terrorism." In addition, the *Wall Street Journal* noted that Lipper "was forced to slash the value of its holdings after concluding that the value of its securities had tumbled and wouldn't recover anytime soon." The *Journal* went on to say that Lipper had decided to value its securities more conservatively. However, other convertible bond arbitrageurs did not run into the same trouble in accurately pricing their portfolios, even though they were trading the same securities.

Pricing the securities in a portfolio requires a third-party source. Once prices, and subsequently, market values, for each of the securities have been obtained, a comparison to the market values supplied by the prime broker for the particular account can be completed, with any material discrepancy investigated by the fund of funds manager. If, for some reason, a security cannot be priced by a third party source, it is imperative to document the price used and the method by which it was obtained.

STYLE DRIFT CASE STUDY: INTEGRAL

The Art Institute of Chicago's highly publicized losses in hedge funds offer a perfect example of how ensuring adherence to investment manager guidelines can reduce the risk of asset loss due to style drift. During the summer of 2000, the Institute was introduced to Integral Investment Management L.P., run by Conrad Seghers and James Dickey. Integral, whose investments were generally in equity, equity derivatives, bonds, and other liquid securities, had been quite successful since launching its funds in 1998. The Institute, as part of its decision to invest in hedge funds, invested $23 million in late 2000 and early 2001, and an additional $20 million in September 2001 in funds managed by Integral. In October 2001, the news regarding the Institute's investments in Integral took a turn for the worse: Integral notified investors that one of their funds, Integral Hedging, had lost close to 90 percent of its value, including $20 million of the Institute's money. Integral blamed the loss on Morgan Stanley, their prime broker, saying that there was a glitch in Morgan Stanley's trading system. This glitch, according to court papers filed in Dallas, caused Morgan Stanley's system to miscalculate the amount of leverage. As prices of the securities dropped, Integral was forced to increase the amount of collateral securing the loans by Morgan, but could not immediately do so. This, according to Integral, caused Morgan Stanley to sell a number of the securities in the portfolio to raise cash. Compounding the problem was the drastic drop in prices after the September 11 terrorists attacks, which caused Morgan to liquidate even more of the portfolio. Morgan Stanley denied it had any computer problems.

Not satisfied with Integral's explanation of what happened, the Institute decided to investigate what occurred on its own. According to the *Wall Street Journal*, the museum discovered that in mid-October, Integral had invested around $17 million in Recovery Partners II, managed by Thornton Capital Advisors, which bought and sold bad consumer debt, including past-due credit card and utility bills. The *Journal* reported that, according to A. Steven Crown, the museum's finance committee chairman, Integral never disclosed "that they intended to invest the plaintiff's funds in such high-risk investments as distressed credit-card debt." But an attorney for Integral, Lawrence J. Friedman, said Mr. Seghers "could have bet on the Super Bowl if he wanted," according to the *Journal*.

This type of disconnect frequently is due to hedge fund managers' stating that they have a specific strategy and invest in specific types of securities (e.g., equity long/short investing in common stocks) during the marketing process, while presenting an offering memorandum—a document supplied to prospective investors detailing the fund's objectives, fees, structure, and so on—that is much more vague and less restrictive (e.g., the fund seeks to achieve capital preservation by investing in securities *primarily* on publicly traded or over-the-counter markets). The fund of funds manager can eliminate these types of problems by outlining, via an investment manager agreement, the specific securities in which the manager of the separate account can invest.

However, it is important to note that if the fund of funds invests its capital into a fund rather than into a separate account, it will be difficult to ensure compliance, since ultimately the investors in the manager's funds are partners in, not owners of, the fund. Furthermore, if investments are made into a fund and the guidelines of the fund are violated, it is difficult to take any quick corrective actions due to lockups and redemption notice periods. However, if the manager of a separate account violated an investment guideline, the fund of funds manager could immediately instruct the manager to take corrective action, direct the prime broker to liquidate positions, or hire another fund manager with a similar style to manage the portfolio.

RISK MANAGEMENT

The following series of questions comes from the AIMA Illustrative Questionnaire for Due Diligence of Fund of Funds Managers (see Appendix A) and pertains to the measures and means in place to monitor and quantify investment risk.

Does the company maintain a written risk management policy? If yes, provide a copy.

Funds of funds will approach risk management differently depending on overall investment philosophy and the degree of transparency available from the underlying hedge funds. For example, the risk management of a fund of funds with a high degree of hedge fund transparency may involve daily independent position pricing and exposure screens. This approach is used to ensure independent verification of hedge fund compliance with the specified investment guidelines. On the other hand, a fund of funds without access to position-level data may conduct its risk management through a monthly or quarterly conference call with each hedge fund manager, relying on manager representations concerning exposures, valuation, and trading activity. In all cases, investors will want to understand how risks are identified and what actions are taken to reduce unwanted risk.

What risk management concepts does the firm apply to its portfolios?

The risk management that a fund of funds manager can apply to a portfolio is limited by its level of access to information and ability to take action to protect the portfolio. The manager must first become aware of a risk issue. Once aware, it must be able to do something about it in order to manage the risk. The earlier this occurs, of course, the better. Ideally, the risk can be avoided altogether. However, in addition to awareness of the problems, there needs to be an ability to take action to contain or eliminate the risk. Where one is invested in a hedge fund rather than a managed account, there is no ability to instruct the manager to make portfolio changes, so the only option is to redeem. This may not take place in time to avoid exposure to the risk. A fund of funds rides the fortunes of the hedge fund in which it invests. If that entity has little or no transparency, the fund of funds manager must rely on the hedge fund manager to report risk situations that arise, or find out by way of third-party rumor. Without any clear knowledge of risk issues, there is no basis upon which to take action.

When a fund of funds manager has knowledge of risk issues, through disclosures by the hedge fund or through an independent evaluation of the portfolio, it still must have the ability to take responsive action or cause the hedge fund manager to take action. If such ability does not exist, then the best the fund of funds can do is to take its money out at the next opportunity allowed by the hedge fund.

When hedge funds agree to operate under established investment guidelines and allow for independent verification, the hedge fund becomes subject to the oversight and accountability necessary for true risk management. Within such a structure, not only is the fund of funds manager aware of any investment guideline violations as soon as they occur, but can also instruct the hedge fund manager to adjust the portfolio to put it back into compliance. For example, consider a hedge fund that operates subject to investment guidelines. One of the guidelines limits leverage to 2:1—for every dollar invested, the fund can borrow another dollar, but no more. If the hedge fund goes outside these bounds and leverages 210 percent, a number of things happen. First, the fund of funds manager is made aware of this risk violation through an independent check. Second, the fund of funds manager can notify the hedge fund manager of the violation and direct him to take action to reduce the 10 percent in excess leverage and bring it back into guideline compliance. "Nipping it in the bud" prevents small increases in unacceptable risk from becoming major issues, such as leverage moving unchecked to 400 percent or 600 percent.

Funds of funds that do not have access to information or recourse to action will manage risk through manager and strategy diversification. Minimum numbers of managers and maximum allocations may be used to limit exposure to any one manager.

Describe the firm's quantitative risk management tools. Provide examples, where available.
A wide variety of information can be evaluated quantitatively. Most work is done evaluating periodic return information. Usually, this is available on a monthly basis, although weekly and daily data

is becoming more prevalent. Analysis usually centers on the risk taken for possible return. Volatility, correlation, and other factors are applied to hedge funds as a stand-alone investment and as a component in a portfolio. Knowing to what extent these measures exceed normal or expected bounds is important for adjusting the portfolio. Many funds of funds will have a range of volatility as a portfolio objective. In order to achieve this, the fund of funds would need to have the tools in place to monitor overall volatility, as well as the contribution of each of the underlying hedge funds. To manage the volatility, the fund of funds must reduce or eliminate investments in some hedge funds and increase or add investments to others depending on the correlation to other portfolio holdings and contribution to overall portfolio volatility. More sophisticated risk management tools are used when funds of funds managers have access to position-level data. These systems allow for pricing of the securities and checking concentration and leverage. Value at Risk (VAR) systems are also becoming more widely used, as daily position-level inputs allow for a more useful analysis. In all cases, it is important to verify that the fund of funds has the tools in place to support its risk management policy.

Does the firm apply leverage to some or all of its products? If so, please explain.

A fund of funds manager can borrow at the fund of funds level to increase the exposure to its underlying hedge funds. For example, a fund of funds with $100 million in investor capital might borrow $50 million to increase its investment in hedge funds. The return of the fund of funds will be the net profit or loss generated by the $150 million investment in the hedge funds less the cost of borrowing the $50 million (and, of course, all fund of funds fees and expenses). If the return on the $150 million is 10 percent, and the cost of borrowing is 4 percent, the return would be $15 million minus $2 million borrowing cost, $13 million (before fund of funds expenses and fees) or 13 percent return. By leveraging, the fund of funds manager increased performance by 3 percent. Conversely, if the return were -10 percent on the $150 million investment, the total return would be -$15 million minus -$2 million borrowing cost for a total loss of -$17 million or -17 percent. This is 7 percent worse than the return on an unleveraged investment. The ideal candidates for leveraging are portfolios that produce returns above the cost of borrowing with a high degree of consistency and good downside protection.

Most fund of funds managers do not use leverage at the fund of funds level as part of their investment approach. Others allow for it, but use it sparingly, usually to manage capital flows and hedge fund liquidity mismatches.

Does the firm maintain a firm-wide risk management system including operational, legal, reputational, and business risks? If so, please describe.

A fund of funds with a stated risk management policy requires a firm-wide system to ensure that the objectives of the policy are achieved. All aspects of the fund of funds activities can and do influence the safety and performance of the fund of funds. Operationally, the movement of investments in and out of the fund of funds includes risks of time lines, accuracy, tax treatment, and fraud. Legally, risks include compliance with securities laws, tax authorities, and other regulators such as the CFTC (Commodities Futures Trading Commission) or Comptroller of the Currency. Reputationally, risks include association in unsavory, avoidable situations.

The overall negative impact to an investor can range from small inconveniences to major problems such as delays in information and return of capital when a fund of funds suspends redemptions and becomes illiquid. Certain legal and regulatory issues can result in lawsuits and fines that are a direct cost to the fund of funds. Unknown and unintended negative tax consequences can be a major problem to taxable and tax-exempt investors alike. And, losses from theft or fraud may also arise. An overall system to integrate the management of overall and department-specific risks is an essential part of a fund of funds operation.

COMPLIANCE AND LEGAL ISSUES

This series of questions addresses what kind of oversight the fund of funds has in place to ensure that the rules and regulations of the various regulatory bodies are being complied with. This due diligence consideration is important for a number of reasons, including that since the assets are commingled, issues that arise either from a regulatory body or from an outside investor will affect all of the investors in the fund.

Is the firm registered with any regulatory and/or supervisory bodies?

In the United States, the most common registration for a fund of funds manager would be as an investment adviser. Registration can take place at the federal level with the Securities and Exchange Commission or at the state level. Most funds of funds have the requisite $25 million under management, which qualifies them for federal registration. If a fund of funds is involved in investing in futures or hedge funds that trade futures (i.e., those involving Commodity Trading Advisors), the fund of funds may also be required to register as a Commodity Pool Operator (CPO). Registration requires following regulations concerning operations, procedures, and record keeping. Certain information about the fund of funds must be filed with the SEC, and specified disclosure information must be provided to clients. Registrants are also subject to periodic regulatory audits.

When was the last SEC inspection?

The SEC audits its registrants every few years. It will review files and activities and check for compliance with SEC rules and regulation. At the conclusion of the on-site visit, preliminary findings of any deficiencies will be discussed with fund of funds management. Within a few months thereafter, a written deficiency letter will be sent to the fund of funds outlining areas in which the registrant appears to be out of compliance. A fund of funds may choose to challenge or discuss a deficiency finding further, but in most cases the issues are easily resolved and changes implemented. If a material violation has occurred, or if a continuing deficiency exists, the SEC may recommend an enforcement action against the fund of funds.

Are any lawsuits pending against the company?
Commercial lawsuits can be a normal part of doing business in the United States. However, in the investment area they are of particular concern when they have a material impact on the functioning of the fund of funds management company, such as when a judgment can endanger the financial viability of the company. Lawsuits claiming misconduct of the firm or personnel associated with current and future investment activities, such as claims of fraud or misappropriation of fund assets, are also hazardous. Regulatory action and criminal charges should be of very high concern as well. Claims and allegations may not be based in fact, but they certainly, at a minimum, highlight areas for additional scrutiny.

Does the company have a full-time compliance officer?
The compliance burden of a fund of funds manager is substantial. The firm needs to follow the rules and regulations of the regulatory bodies that it answers to. It is also subject to the laws of the various jurisdictions in which it does business. Compliance with these requirements involves filings, record keeping, disclosures, and reporting. Such requirements also specify how fund of funds products can be sold and what qualifications an investor must have to be able to invest in the fund of funds. Coordinating these requirements throughout the firm can be a complex task. In order to accomplish it, a fund of funds will usually designate an individual to act as compliance officer. The compliance officer coordinates both with outside attorneys, advisers, and regulators and with the various departments of the firm to establish policies and procedures to ensure that the broad range of compliance issues and requirements are satisfied.

Does the company have a written compliance manual? If yes, please provide a copy.
The policies and procedures followed by the fund of funds to ensure compliance with external rules and regulations, as well as

internal controls, are normally set forth in writing. In some instances, it may be a collection of the controls followed by each department, but in most cases there should be a centralization of the processes to ensure coordination.

Provide a list of professional counterparties with which the firm maintains a business relationship. These typically include the following:
■ Custodians
■ Administrators
■ Legal advisers
■ Auditors
■ Banks
■ Distribution channels
■ External marketers
■ Other important business partners

A fund of funds will receive professional services from some or all of the entities listed above. It is important to understand whom a fund of funds works with and how they fit into the overall functioning and operations of the fund of funds. Ask for contacts at these businesses as another source of references.

How does the firm ensure an alignment of interests between the firm (as fund manager) and the investor? How much of the firm's or the partners' money is invested in the firm's products? Are there any conflicts of interests the investor should be aware of?
Investors are looking to invest in a fund of funds that strives to deliver top performance within stated objectives and constraints. There is an inherent alignment of interests in that better-performing funds of funds will attract more assets, and therefore generate more management fees. Investors should examine the structure of the fund of funds and the fund of funds management company to determine incentive structures of key individuals. If the fund of funds manager and portfolio managers are compensated based on fund of funds' performance, they have an incentive to continually seek to improve

performance. When the fund of funds' manager's employees share in firm profits, all have an incentive to improve their efficiency and fund performance. Incentive and stock option programs tend to help retain key employees, adding to the stability and consistency of the management of the fund of funds.

An investment of the fund of funds' manager's money in the fund of funds alongside the investor's capital demonstrates a somewhat direct alignment, putting the manager in an investor's position and demonstrating a willingness by the manager to "eat one's own cooking." Overall, the investor's interest and the fund of funds manager's interests are never fully aligned, and conflicts of interest always exist. For example, the fund of funds may invest in hedge funds that the manager has an ownership interest in, or he may earn stock or futures brokerage commissions on trading by some of the underlying hedge funds. The existence of such arrangements gives funds of funds managers an incentive to allocate money to a hedge fund from which they may profit via fees or commissions over a hedge fund that might otherwise be a more promising performer. Such conflicts indicate the potential for a lack of alignment. These types of conflicts are normally detailed in disclosures in the offering memorandum. When the disclosures are vague or absent, an investor should inquire about their existence directly. By doing so, investors are put on notice that the issues exist and can investigate further to make an informed decision as to whether they wish to invest under such circumstances.

SUMMARY

Prudent investors seek to determine the level of risk management that a fund of funds employs. Distinctions should be made between efforts to become aware of risks or monitor risk versus the employment of actual risk management operations whereby action can be taken to eliminate unacceptable risks. Much of this depends on the philosophy and manner of investment, centering around the degree of transparency and management of portfolios. Investors should also evaluate controls on operations and compliance, degree of regulatory oversight, and the use of and competency of service providers.

Fund of Funds Selection Case Study 11

T O PULL TOGETHER the selection process detailed in the preceding chapters, what follows is its application in a hypothetical case study featuring a U.S. foundation. In getting to the fund of funds selection stage, the investment staff of the foundation has educated its members about the hedge fund industry, as discussed in Parts 1 and 2 of this book, and has retained expert advisers to consult on the subject. After evaluating the merits of adding hedge funds to its traditional portfolio, a decision to move ahead is made.

SCENARIO

A medium-sized foundation with some $200 million in assets has decided to invest approximately $20 million, or 10 percent of its assets, in hedge funds. The foundation has a small investment staff and investment committee. The investment team has decided to invest in a fund of funds rather than investing directly in individual hedge fund managers. Working with its consultant, the foundation begins by setting its objectives and parameters, as discussed in Chapter 7.

STEP 1: DEFINING INVESTMENT OBJECTIVES AND PARAMETERS

The objectives that the foundation identifies are to gain *diversified* exposure to a range of hedge fund exposures and to achieve stable, risk-adjusted returns with volatility less than one-half that of the S&P 500 (using a simple measure such as a Sharpe Ratio above 1 and maximum drawdown of 8 percent) and a low correlation to the S&P 500 of 0.5. The fund of funds firm should have more than $100 million in assets under management and have at least a three-year track record. The parameters established specify that the fund of funds must be for U.S. tax-exempt investors, have quarterly liquidity with less than 60-days notice, and have fees at or below the industry average.

The key objectives and parameters for the fund of funds to be selected are summarized as follows:

Objectives:
■ Fund of Funds Portfolio Construction: Diversified
■ Performance: Above benchmark
■ Volatility (standard): Less than one-half that of the S&P 500 index
■ Maximum Drawdown (loss): 8 percent
■ Correlation to S&P 500: Less than 0.5
■ Benchmark: HFRX Global Index

Parameters:
■ Investor Type: Tax-exempt, U.S.
■ Liquidity: Monthly
■ Lockup: None
■ Fees: Average or less
■ Minimum three-year track record
■ Minimum $100 million under management
■ Experienced investment team with a well-defined manager selection and due diligence process
■ Strong risk controls, as the investor has fiduciary obligations and is concerned about reputational risk

■ Good client communication, as the investment staff has to report regularly to the foundation's investment committee, and quarterly reports have to be prepared for the foundation's board of directors

STEP 2: SCREENING TO CREATE THE FUNDS OF FUNDS SHORT LIST

Using the third-party funds of funds database and adding some funds of funds known to the investment staff and its consultant, a universe of five hundred funds of funds is established. Using the above objectives and parameters, this universe is screened.

After conducting a general screen, followed by a more detailed screen, a short list of ten promising candidates, managers A-J, is produced. Each fund of funds manager on this short list satisfies the screenable objectives and parameters. Ten is a manageable number of funds of funds for the foundation staff and its consultant to evaluate in more detail.

STEP 3: CONDUCTING A DUE DILIGENCE SCREEN OF THE FUNDS OF FUNDS SHORT LIST

The foundation contacts the ten funds of funds on the short list and begins the due diligence process by sending out a Request for Proposal (RFP), which included a fund of funds due diligence questionnaire. The responses are received and evaluated, as discussed in Chapters 7–10. In the answers provided by the ten candidates, some questions were lacking in detail, and in response to a follow-up call, one fund of funds is resistant to providing the necessary level of detail required. Two of the funds of funds, in providing further detail, do not actually satisfy parameter criteria. The remaining seven provide detailed and satisfactory responses, although some appear stronger than others. Site visits are arranged with each of the seven remaining fund of funds management companies. During the visits, the strengths and weaknesses of each firm become even more apparent, and they clearly fall into two groups, with three showing much stronger than the remaining four. These three funds of funds are selected as finalists.

STEP 4: EVALUATING FINALISTS FOR SELECTION

A summary of each of the three finalists is prepared and presented to the investment committee for consideration.

Manager A. Eight-year track record, $2.6 billion under management. This fund of funds has strong absolute returns, with top quartile performance since inception compared to other funds of funds and to a hedge fund industry index. Manager A has significant assets under management, a list of top institutions as investors, and a large staff with more than ten investment professionals dedicated to fund of funds investment research, due diligence, and portfolio construction. The firm's three principals each have eight to ten years of experience in managing fund of funds investments. In addition, Manager A has a rigorous manager selection process, uses robust portfolio construction methodology, and receives monthly exposure reports from the hedge fund managers in which it invests. Manager A is unlikely to allocate a significant amount of time to specific data or information requests by the investor, given that its investment is likely to only be approximately 1 percent of Manager A's assets and unlikely to grow substantially. Manager A does, however, provide all investors a fairly detailed quarterly report on the fund's strategy allocation and a summary of investment performance.

Investigation into Manager A's track record reveals, however, that the first four years of the fund of funds' existence account for most of its superior investment performance. Over the past several years Manager A's performance has steadily declined against the peer group and industry benchmarks. Indeed, in the last two years Manager A's performance has been a bit below the industry average.

Further investigation reveals that Manager A's main fund is currently invested in sixty-three hedge fund managers, and was during its first two years invested in just six managers, one of which constituted about 30 percent of the allocation of Manager A's fund of funds. This single fund, Multistrategy Hedge Fund LLP, was a star performer and was responsible for more than 50 percent of Manager A's net return during the first three years of its tenure. Multistrategy Hedge Fund LLP has been closed to new investment for the past three years, and its performance has been about average during the last two years. As Manager A's fund of funds has grown from approximately $400 million in assets four years ago to over $2 billion in assets today, Multistrategy Hedge Fund LLP has dwindled to 5 percent of Manager A's fund of funds allocation.

Summary Consideration. Some funds of funds have built strong track records on the backs of a few well-chosen manager picks. The investor must try to determine if this outperformance was fortuitous or is likely to be replicated in the future.

Outperformance generated by concentrated manager allocations tends to decline as a fund of funds' assets grow and the fund of funds is required to invest in an ever-larger pool of managers. In addition, as hedge fund managers with superior investment performance attract assets, they eventually reach capacity and close to new investment. Many have strong historical records but have underperformed in recent years. Some funds of funds use their investment in marquee hedge fund managers as a selling point to prospective investors. Even if a fund of funds has reserved some capacity with these marquee managers, however, even if they continue to be top performers, it usually does not keep pace with the overall growth in the fund of funds manager's assets, and every new dollar into the fund of funds dilutes the exposure. Also, manager outperformance persistence is rare, and an allocation decision based on access to a manager may not meet objectives and parameter requirements.

To stay ahead of the fund of funds industry average, a fund of funds must consistently be able to do one or both of the following: (1) pick managers in strategies that will outperform going forward and (2) advantageously over/underweight strategies to invest in them in sufficient size to positively affect the fund of funds' investment return. It is not an easy job to pick even a few hedge fund managers who will outperform their peers going forward. It is an even more difficult task to successfully pick more than fifty managers who will outperform their peers. Persistence of superior returns by funds of funds, then, tends to be fleeting. The fate of many funds of funds with top investment returns based on the performance of early years is likely to be similar to that of top-performing equity mutual funds: reversion to the mean and a long, inexorable rendez-vous with mediocre investment returns.

Manager B. Six-year track record, $1 billion under management. This fund of funds also has strong absolute returns, with top quartile performance compared to other funds of funds and a hedge fund industry index. The fund has done particularly well over the last two-year period. Manager B has a staff of six investment professionals dedicated to fund of funds investment research, due diligence, and portfolio construction. Manager B meets the investor's other requirements on risk control and client service.

Due diligence by the investor reveals that Manager B's chief investment officer (CIO), who had more than twelve years of experience in evaluating and investing in hedge fund managers and was well regarded in the industry, left the firm about a year and a half ago. He had been with the firm since inception and was largely responsible for its manager selection and portfolio construction process. Manager B's CEO and founder has spent most of his time in recent years marketing the firm and its funds and managing the business. Manager B has hired a well-qualified replacement for its departed CIO. In addition, the firm has four analysts, two of whom have been with the firm three years and have five years of industry experience, and two of whom have been hired over the last year by the new CIO.

Summary Consideration. An investor needs to determine the strength of a fund of funds' manager selection process and the people making the investment decisions. Just as a fund of funds manager tries to determine for a hedge fund who currently makes, and who historically has made, the investment decisions for the fund, an investor should try to determine the consistency of a fund of funds' investment process and the strength of those who are making the investment decisions for the fund of funds.

In the example above, the strong performance of Manager B might be the result of the intelligence and judgment of the departed chief investment officer (CIO). This would seem to be the case for the first four years of the fund of funds' existence. It may or may not be the case for the last year or two. The firm, however, could be running on fumes; that is, the strong manager picks and strategy allocation of the departed CIO might continue to be responsible for the favorable investment returns. Alternatively, the strong recent performance may also be due in part to the contributions of the new CIO and the increasingly experienced analyst team. This would require further due diligence. How much of the manager selection and allocation process is based on the work product and discretion of the CIO? How much is incorporated into the firm's investment operation procedures? Having a one-on-one with the new CIO, and gaining an understanding of the fund of funds' investment process before and after the departure of the CIO, are good places to start. Also, understanding the fund of funds' research and portfolio management process will help the investor form an opinion as to the likelihood that Manager B will continue to produce above-average investment returns going forward.

Manager C. Seven-year track record and $500 million under management. Manager C also has fairly good returns and has outperformed the fund of funds industry over the past three years. Manager C has a staff of eight investment professionals and a team of three client service specialists who communicate well with current and prospective investors. A large investment bank acquired Manager C two years ago. The CEO of Manager C previously headed the alternative investment operation of a large corporate pension fund. He has now been appointed head of Manager C's parent firm's institutional hedge fund platform.

Manager C has a strong investment process, an experienced and motivated investment team, and a strong client orientation. The firm sponsors two well-regarded symposiums on hedge fund investing each year. Representatives of Manager C have helped the investor to better understand and to feel more comfortable with investing in hedge funds.

Additional due diligence by the investor reveals that about 60 percent of the hedge fund managers currently in Manager C's fund of funds use Manager C's firm (parent company) for prime broker-age. This is up from about 20 percent three years ago. Manager C's parent company is a significant provider of prime brokerage services to hedge funds. The hedge funds in Manager C's fund of funds that use its prime brokerage services have on average done better than the other hedge funds in Manager C's portfolio.

Summary Consideration. Fund of funds, like practically all investment firms, at some level have conflicts of interest. An investor needs to figure out what these are and determine how significant a negative effect they may have on the investor's ultimate goal: superior investment returns.

With hedge funds and funds of funds having gone mainstream over the past five years, a number of fund of funds players have been and will continue to be bought up by larger industry money management firms. As with any acquisition, the acquiree undergoes a period of stress when being integrated into another organization, which may have its own priorities and ways of operating. Like all firms, however, the bottom line is usually maximizing profits, and this does not always work to the advantage of an investor.

In the scenario above, although the evidence is not conclusive, there may be some internal dynamic causing Manager C's fund of funds to gravitate toward using hedge fund managers that use Manager C's prime brokerage services. Prime brokerage is a very lucrative business for Manager C's parent. It could be something as simple as Manager C's firm being a top prime broker that attracts institutional-quality hedge funds, or that the prime brokerage group of Manager C does a good job of promoting its hedge fund clients to the fund of funds community, including its in-house fund.

The concern, of course, is that there is a conflict of interest, and whether consciously or unconsciously, the senior management of Manager C is, all things being equal, favoring hedge funds that generate revenue for Manager C's parent company. Increased revenue is sure to please the head office management who oversee Manager C. Although so far the hedge funds using Manager C's prime brokerage services have done well, the question is whether Manager C would be more hesitant to terminate or redeem assets from these managers in the event they underperform. That said, Manager C's other strengths may outweigh the concern over the prime brokerage issue.

A similar dynamic can come into play with funds of funds that sponsor start-up hedge funds, where the fund of funds typically takes a percentage of equity of the hedge fund's management or incentive fee in exchange for funding the manager and/or providing it management or marketing services. A conflict exists in that the fund of funds has a business incentive to keep fund of funds assets with the manager, even when better manager choices may be available elsewhere.

FINAL SELECTIONS

After some additional investigation, the foundation's investment committee selects a fund of funds for investment: Manager B is the choice. Manager A was eliminated because, although it had strong performance and a long history, the returns in recent years were below par. Also, the investment management presentation relied heavily on access to star managers rather than demonstrating strength in identifying new talent and shifting allocations to more favorable strategies. In addition, Manager A's level of risk management was minimal, and the firm had little or no access to verified portfolio information on the managers in which it invested.

Manager C was eliminated based on its shift toward predominantly using managers at its affiliated prime broker. One positive aspect noted was access to position-level information from these funds. Overweighing this benefit, however, were two critical factors. First, the strength of the prime broker was in equities. The move toward more managers at the affiliated prime broker resulted in less strategy diversification in the fund of funds. Although equities were doing well at the time, the reduction in diversification was seen as a departure from historical portfolio management practices that could result in higher volatility and greater losses when the equity environment changed. Second, while Manager C had a higher level of information access than Manager A, the business conflicts indicated that there might be limited internal challenge to investment activities and position pricing practices—after all, the hedge fund managers in which

Manager C invested represented billions of dollars of fee-generating assets to the parent company's prime brokerage business, well beyond that of the fund of fund allocation of Manager C.

Although Manager B had experienced a change in CIO eighteen months ago, the due diligence indicated that much of the firm's portfolio management strength came from its ability to access and process information about the hedge fund manager's investment activities and analyze strategy performance prospects. Much of this was due to Manager B's infrastructure as well as the collective work of a number of other talented individuals at the firm. The new CIO easily stepped into the position, and because of the depth of information and the quality of research generated by the firm, was able to continue to generate strong performance. This view was re-inforced by the fact that the former CIO's performance in his new position was below the industry average. As another plus, Manager B had recently taken steps to raise the level of transparency required from its managers, and had integrated this higher level of information into its risk management and strategy allocation processes.

SUMMARY

This case study ends in a final fund of funds selection. But in practice, the selection decision is just the end of the beginning. The fund of funds investment must be monitored for its compliance with the foundation's investment parameters and its ability to meet the foundation's investment objectives. The investment is also evaluated against competition, both in terms of performance as well as features such as transparency and risk management, reporting, liquidity, and fees. The hedge fund industry is dynamic and evolving. Most developments are in the direction of providing higher levels of service and better terms for investors, and a wider range of investment products designed to more precisely satisfy the requirements of client types. Further, the level of education and knowledge in the industry among advisers, consultants, and investors in general has advanced significantly. The result is better opportunities and decisions in selection and investing in funds of funds.

Appendix A

AIMA Due Diligence Questionnaire

AIMA's Illustrative Questionnaire
for Due Diligence of

FUND OF FUNDS MANAGERS

Published by
The Alternative Investment Management Association Limited (AIMA)

AIMA's Illustrative Questionnaire for Due Diligence Review of
FUND OF FUNDS MANAGERS

The purpose of this document is to serve as a guide to investors in their relations with fund of funds managers. This due diligence questionnaire is an unavoidable process that investors must follow in order to choose a manager.

Not all of the following questions are applicable to all managers but we recommend that you ask as many questions as possible before making a decision.

DISCLAIMER

Whilst AIMA has used all reasonable efforts to produce a questionnaire of general application in connection with a due diligence appraisal of fund of funds managers, in any particular case an investor is likely to have its own individual requirements and each fund of funds manager its own characteristics. As a result, prior to any individual investor sending out the questionnaire, it is strongly recommended that the questions are reviewed and, where necessary, amended to suit its own requirements and its state of knowledge of the fund of funds manager's operations.

In addition, responses to the questionnaire should not be relied upon without review and, where considered appropriate, further investigation. In order to obtain the best possible information on any specific fund of funds manager additional questions should be raised to clarify any point of uncertainty, and where practicable verbal examination should be undertaken. In particular, AIMA recommends that in respect of special areas of concern, such as fund performance or risk profile, independent third party data should, if possible, be obtained in order to verify these facts.

Accordingly, none of AIMA, its officers, employees or agents make any representation or warranty, express or implied, as to the adequacy, completeness or correctness of the questionnaire. No liability whatsoever is accepted by AIMA, its officers, employees or agents for any loss howsoever arising from any use of this questionnaire or its contents or otherwise arising in connection therewith.

Other AIMA questionnaires available for selection of:
Managed Futures Managers
Fund of Funds Custody and Administration
Hedge Fund Administration (excl. Fund of Funds) for Managers
Hedge Fund Administration (excl. Fund of Funds) for Investors
Hedge Fund Managers
Prime Brokers

AIMA's Illustrative Questionnaire for Due Diligence Review of
FUND OF FUNDS MANAGERS

CONTENTS

Items

Background Information

Product Information

Performance

Asset Allocation/Style Allocation

Due Diligence/Manager Selection

Portfolio Construction

Risk Management

Administration/Operations

Client Information/Reporting

Compliance/Legal

Published by
The Alternative Investment Management Association (AIMA)
Lower Ground Floor, 10 Stanhope Gate, Mayfair, London W1K 1AL
Tel +44 (0)20 7659 9920
Fax +44 (0)20 7659 9921
E-mail: info@aima.org
Web: www.aima.org

BACKGROUND INFORMATION

CONTACT INFORMATION

Company name:
Address:
Telephone:
Fax:
E-mail:
Website:
Name of contacts:
Title of contacts:
Telephone of contacts:

STAFF INFORMATION

E-mail of contacts:
How many employees does the firm currently have?
Show the number of employees by working area:
What is the greatest and least number of employees the firm has had in the last three years?
Explain any significant employee turnover:
How does the firm attract new people?
Provide a brief background of key personnel (education, professional background):
Explain the compensation scheme for key people:

COMPANY STRUCTURE

Legal structure:
Provide details of the firm's current ownership structure and any changes in the last three years:
Are there any plans for further ownership changes?
Provide a short history of the company with the most important milestones:
Provide a chart of the legal structure of the firm and list all branch or affiliate offices:
Provide an organisation chart:

ASSET MANAGEMENT ACTIVITIES

Does the firm conduct any other business than asset management in alternative investments?
State the nature of those other businesses:
Does the firm manage investments of other asset classes (incl. traditional assets), too?
　If so, explain:
Does the firm manage funds of funds in different strategies?
　If so, describe:
What percentage of assets under management is in funds of funds?
Which investor group does the firm primarily target?
Provide a list of main clients (incl. size of assets, duration of client relationship):
Provide three client references:

What are the current assets under management?
- Total
- Traditional
- Alternative

Show the growth of assets under management over the last five years:
- Total
- Traditional
- Alternative

Show a breakdown of assets under management by:
- Client group
- Strategy

What is the greatest percentage of assets under management represented by any single and by the three largest clients?

PRODUCT INFORMATION

Provide a short description of all products (public and private, where disclosure possible) of the firm, e.g. fund of funds, advisory mandates, client portfolios, structured products, etc. Include at least:
- Investment objective (including target return and target risk)
- Target investors
- Legal structure
- Asset allocation
- Number of funds in the portfolio
- Current size
- Date of inception
- Fee structure
- Conditions for Subscriptions and Redemptions

State any other costs and fees borne by the product than the fees mentioned above:

Describe the minimum investment amounts of the different types of products and services:

Does the firm specialist on any product or group of products? If so, please explain:

PERFORMANCE

Provide historical performance data for all products (in electronic form, where possible), including:
- Monthly returns
- Standard deviation (annualised)
- Three largest drawdowns and recovery periods
- Percentage of positive/negative months

State in which period performance is actual or pro forma (backtracked)?

Is performance net of fees to the investor?

ASSET ALLOCATION/STYLE ALLOCATION

Describe the firm's asset allocation process:

On what basis does the firm define and change the asset allocation of the portfolios?

On what periodicity is the asset allocation of the portfolios reviewed?

For non-standard products, to what extent can the investor be involved in the asset allocation process?

Do investment guidelines exist for all products? If so, please provide sample:

How can the guidelines be altered?

DUE DILIGENCE/MANAGER SELECTION

On what principles are the firm's due diligence process based?

Describe in detail the firm's due diligence process. Provide examples of reports and working papers, where available:

Name the minimum requirements (killer criteria) a manager has to meet, if any, to pass the due diligence:

Do you conduct on-site visits with the managers?

How much time is spent with each manager during the due diligence process?
- Before initial investment
- Every following year

How many new managers do you analyse per year? In how many of the analysed managers do you finally invest?

Do you carry out due diligence checks on the administrator or any other service provider to the target investee funds? If so, please describe:

How many managers are currently on your approved list?

How much capacity is available from managers on the approved list? Please provide break-down by strategy:

PORTFOLIO CONSTRUCTION

Explain the qualitative and quantitative criteria used in your portfolio construction process:

State the average turnover of managers within the portfolios:

Does the turnover of managers in different portfolios vary substantially?

What are the main reasons for managers to be excluded from an existing portfolio?

Has a manager included in a portfolio of the firm ever gone out of business due to losses? If yes, what are the lessons learned from that experience and how have they been applied to your business?

Are portfolios transparent to the investor?

How does the firm secure capacity with top class managers now and in the future?

What is the competitive edge in the firm's investment strategy?

How sustainable is this competitive edge?

RISK MANAGEMENT

Does the company maintain a written risk management policy? If yes, provide a copy:

What risk management concepts does the firm apply to its portfolios?

Describe the firm's quantitative risk management tools. Provide examples, where available:

Does the firm apply leverage to some or all of its products? If so, please explain:

Does the firm maintain a firm wide risk management system including operational, legal, reputational and business risks? If so, please describe:

ADMINISTRATION/OPERATIONS

Is the fund administration performed in-house? If performed in-house:
- What are the tasks of the fund administration?
- How often does the firm calculate/estimate the NAVs of the products?
- Does an independent party review those calculations?
- What systems are used for the fund administration?
- Are the computer systems developed in-house or does the company use standard products?

If services are outsourced:
- Which tasks are fulfilled by external service providers (include names of companies)?
- How long have the relationships with those service providers lasted?
- Has the firm ever terminated any service providers (including auditors)? If so, explain the circumstances:

CLIENT INFORMATION/REPORTING

What kinds of reports are sent to investors? Provide sample reports:
Can investors receive customised reports?
What is the periodicity of the reporting?
Are audited reports available to the investor? Provide sample:
Does the company publish regularly in the press? Provide sample:
Has the company published or commissioned any research/academic papers? Provide samples:

COMPLIANCE/LEGAL

Is the firm registered with any regulatory and/or supervisory bodies?
When was the last inspection of those bodies?
Are any lawsuits pending against the company?
Does the company have a full time compliance officer?
Does the company have a written compliance manual? If yes, please provide a copy:
Provide a list of professional counterparties the firm maintains a business relationship with:
- Custodians
- Administrators
- Legal advisors
- Auditors
- Banks
- Distribution channels
- External marketers
- Other important business partners

How does the firm ensure an alignment of interests between the firm, as fund manager, and the investor?
How much of the firm's or the partners' money is invested in the firm's products?
Are there any conflicts of interests the investor should be aware of?

Please attach the most recent disclosure document, information memorandum, and marketing literature.

In the event of amendments to the aforementioned documents, notably the memorandum, please ensure that we will receive those directly from you within reasonable time, as well as copies of proxy's and notification of the Annual General Meeting (the latter only for information purposes).

Please state the name and title of the officer at your firm who has prepared and reviewed this questionnaire.

Name:

Date:

Position:

Appendix B

Excerpts from

HFR Fund of Funds

Industry Report

Hedge Fund Research, Inc. (HFR) is a research firm specializing in the aggre-
gation, dissemination and analysis of alternative investment information. The company produces HFR Database, one of the industry's most widely used commercial
databases of hedge fund performance, as well as a variety of other research products for the alternative investment industry, including the HFR Industry Report. HFR
also produces and distributes the HFRI Monthly Performance Indices—an industry
standard benchmark of hedge fund performance.

HFRI FUND OF FUND INDUSTRY OVERVIEW

Methodology

The estimates contained in this report are based upon HFR Database, which tracks
the hedge fund of funds industry. HFR Database consists of information on over
4,600 single- and multi-strategy funds worldwide. The majority of fund information in the Database is distributed to HFR subscribers, with permission of the fund
managers. Funds that decline to be included in the distributed hedge fund database
are tracked internally by HFR. Asset size and performance for a subset of internally-
tracked funds are determined by internal company estimates and a variety of other
sources.

In order to arrive at the total assets and asset flows by strategy, HFR uses total assets
from all funds contained in the HFRI Fund of Funds Composite Index as well as all
funds tracked internally. The "number of hedge funds" estimates are derived from
internal company estimates and a variety of other sources.

All figures and calculations are based upon information as of June 30, 2003.

HFRI FUND OF FUND INDICES PERFORMANCE AND RISK/RETURN ANALYSIS

HFRI Index Methodology

The HFRI Fund of Fund Indices (HFRI) [*see page 216 and following*] are equally weighted performance indices utilized globally as an Industry benchmark. The Indices are broken into four different categories by strategy, (Conservative, Diversified, Market Defensive, and Strategic) [*see pages 244–251*], including the HFRI Fund of Funds Composite [*see pages 242–243*], which accounts for more than four hundred funds listed on the internal HFR Database.

Funds included in the HFRI Fund of Fund Indices must report in monthly returns, in Net of All Fees returns, and in assets in USD. All HFRI are fund weighted (equal weighted). There is no required asset-size minimum for fund inclusion in the HFRI and no required length of time a fund must be actively trading before inclusion in the HFRI. If a fund liquidates/closes, that fund's performance will be included in the HFRI as of that fund's last reported performance update. Both domestic and offshore funds are included in the HFRI.

The HFRI Indices have been adjusted for survivorship and "instant history" biases.

Calculations

Annualized Returns, Standard Deviation, Sharpe Ratios, Positive Monthly Performance, and correlation to the S&P 500 (with dividends) for each of the HFRI Fund of Fund Indices were calculated over a one, three, five, and twelve-year period based on monthly performance. All Sharpe and Sortino Ratios assume a 5 percent Risk-Free Rate. The Sortino Ratio also assumes a 5 percent MAR (Minimum Acceptable Return). The HFRI Fund of Fund Indices performance is calculated on an annualized yearly and on a five-year monthly basis. The HFRI Fund of Fund Indices performance is also calculated on a growth of $1,000 since 1990 along with a trailing twelve month compounded return. In addition, the growth of $1,000 is calculated on a one, three, and five-year basis. Positive Monthly Performance was calculated by dividing the number of months the HFRI Fund of Fund Indices performed positive over the appropriate time period. The Benchmarks used to compare the HFRI Fund of Fund Indices include the HFRI Fund Weighted Composite Index, S&P 500 (with dividends), and the Lehman Brothers Government/Credit Aggregate Bond Index.

Quarterly performance and 12-Month Moving Average are calculated for each HFRI Index over a five-year period. In addition, each HFRI Index is compared to the benchmarks using Up/Down Capture and Return Distribution Analysis over a five-year period. Up/Down Capture Analysis is performed by calculating the average monthly performance during the "up" and "down" months of the market using the S&P 500 as a benchmark and can be used to compare performance of a particular strategy during both negative and positive performing months of the market. The Return Distribution Analysis is performed by calculating the percentage of monthly average returns over the given time period and can be used to compare the dispersion of returns to the benchmarks.

**HFRI FUND OF FUND
INDUSTRY OVERVIEW**

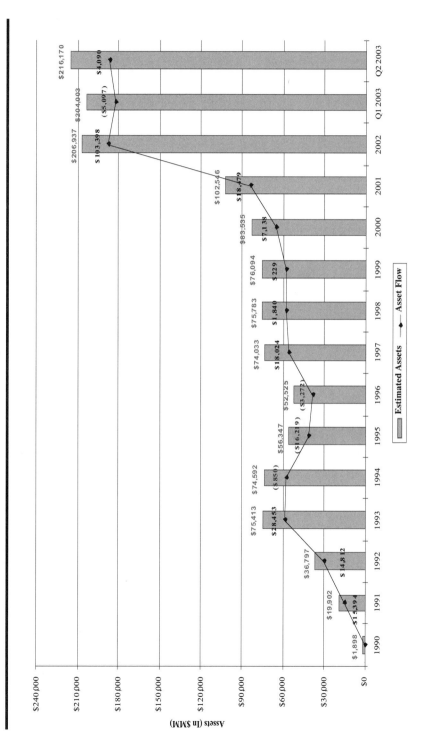

**Estimated Growth of Assets/Asset Flow
Fund of Funds Industry 1990–Q2 2003**

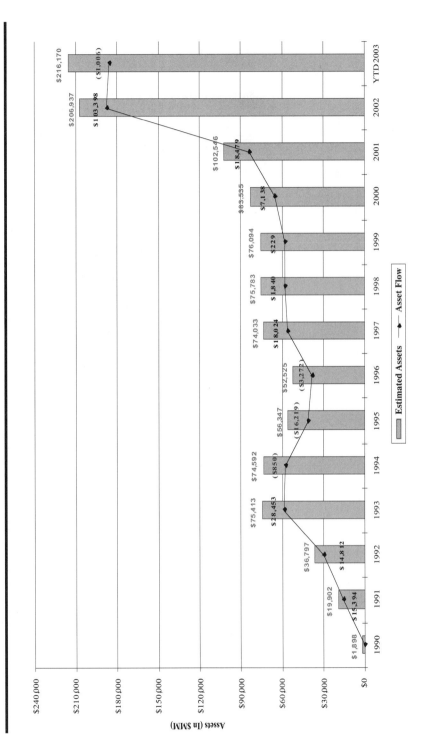

**Estimated Growth of Assets/Asset Flow
Fund of Funds Industry 1990–YTD 2003**

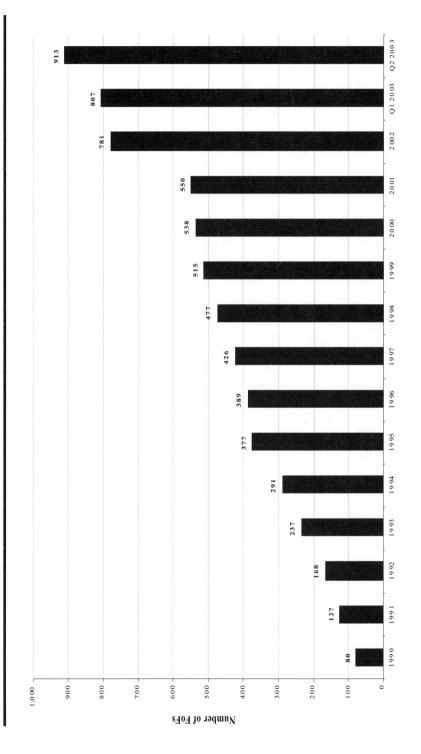

Estimated Number of Funds of Funds
1990–Q2 2003

Estimated Fund of Funds (FOF) Substrategy Composition by Assets Under Management: Q2 2003

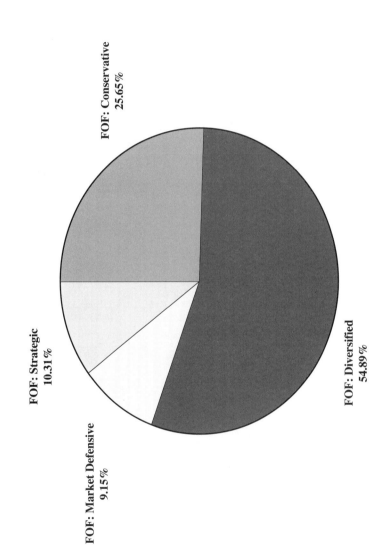

FOF: Conservative
25.65%

FOF: Strategic
10.31%

FOF: Market Defensive
9.15%

FOF: Diversified
54.89%

**Estimated Substrategy Composition
by Number of Funds of Funds: Q2 2003**

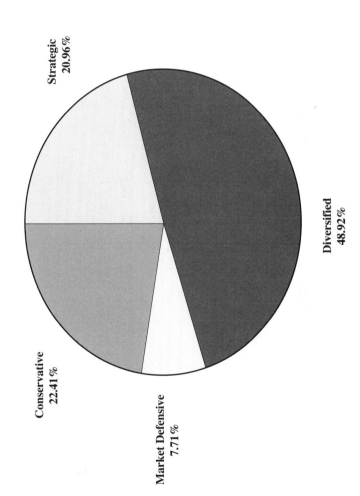

Strategic
20.96%

Diversified
48.92%

Conservative
22.41%

Market Defensive
7.71%

HFRI FUND OF FUND INDICES
PERFORMANCE AND RISK/RETURN ANALYSIS

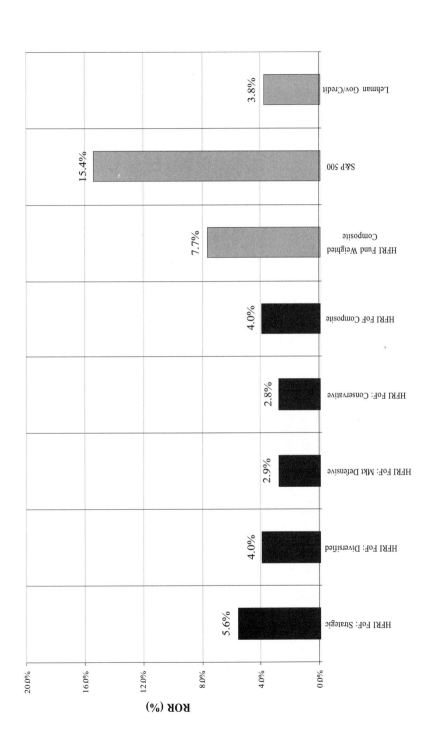

HFRI Fund of Fund Indices Performance Q2 2003

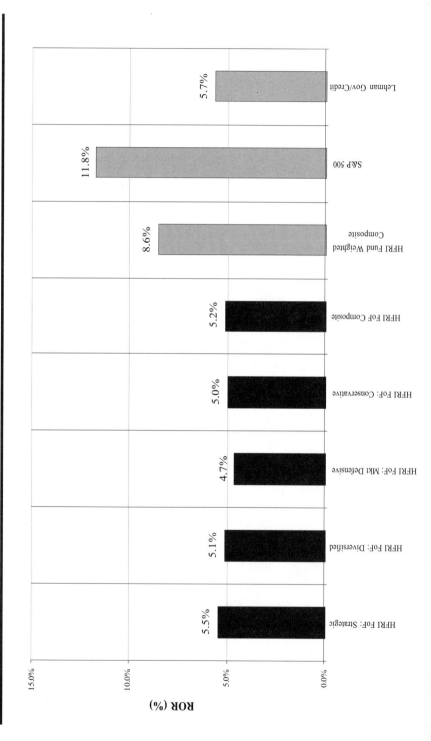

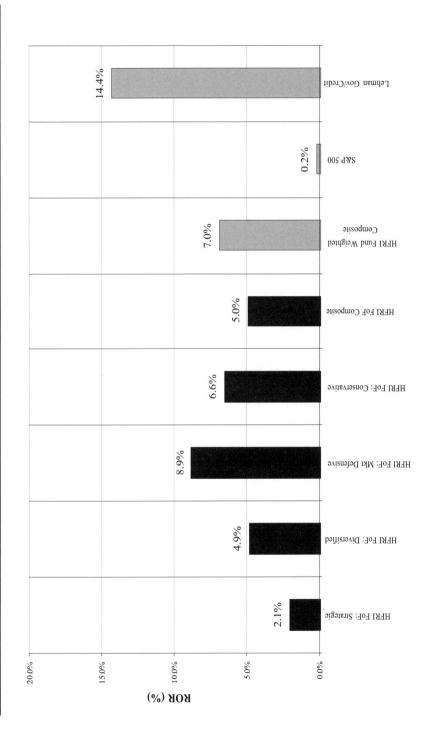

**HFRI Fund of Fund Indices Performance
1 Year Annualized (Q3 2002–Q2 2003)**

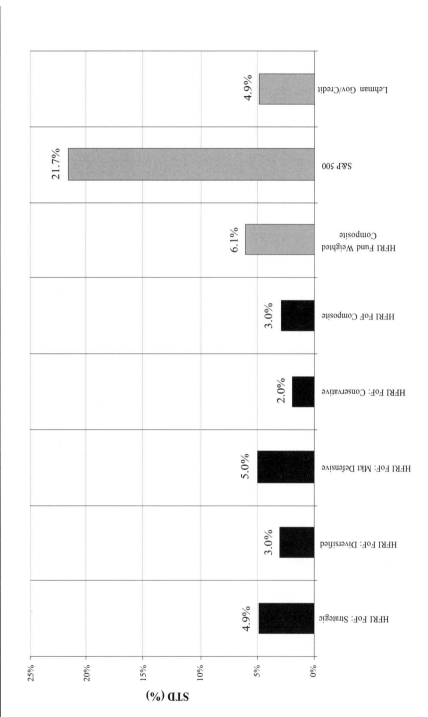

**HFRI Fund of Fund Indices Standard Deviation
1 Year Annualized (Q3 2002–Q2 2003)**

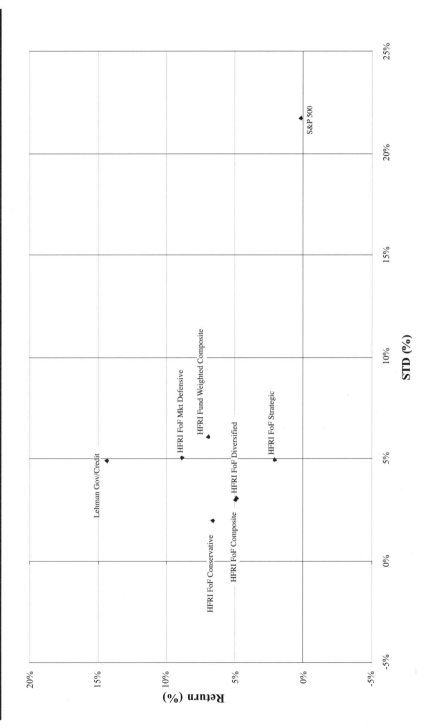

**HFRI Fund of Fund Indices Risk Return Comparison
1 Year Annualized (Q3 2002–Q2 2003)**

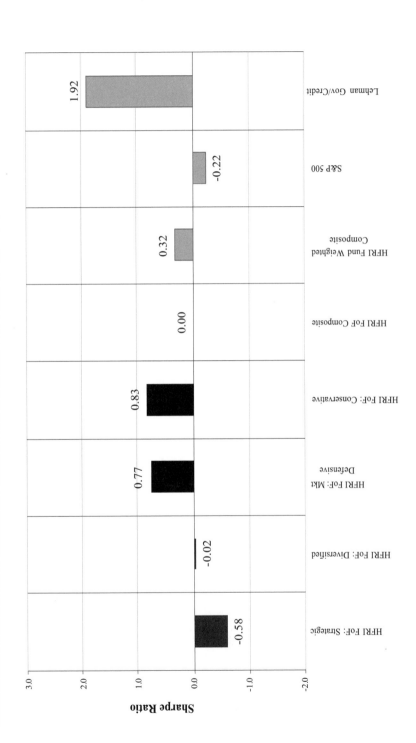

HFRI Fund of Fund Indices Sharpe Ratio
1 Year Annualized (Q3 2002–Q2 2003)

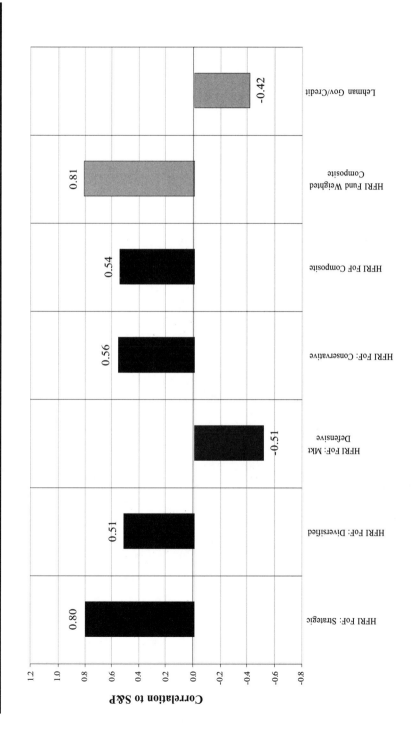

HFRI Fund of Fund Indices Correlation to S&P 500 Index
1 Year Annualized (Q3 2002–Q2 2003)

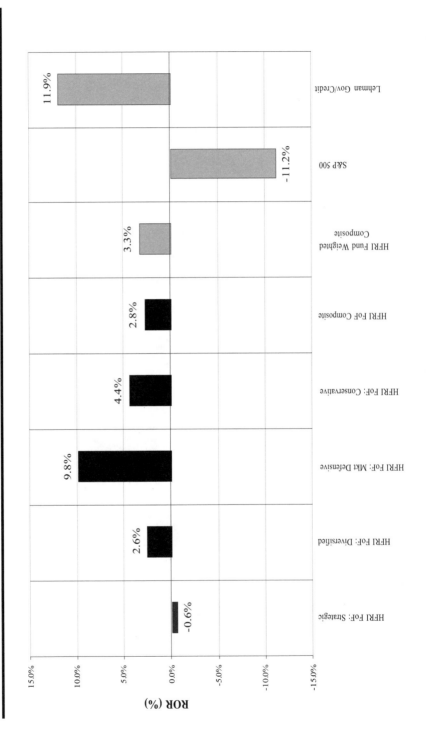

**HFRI Fund of Fund Indices Performance
3 Year Annualized (Q3 2000–Q2 2003)**

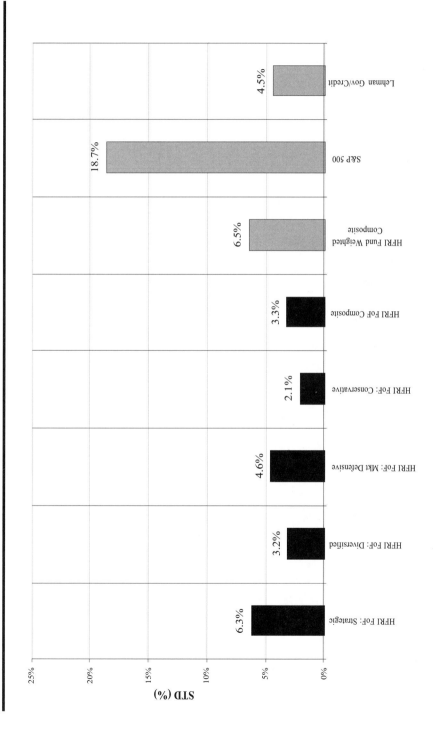

HFRI Fund of Fund Indices Standard Deviation
3 Year Annualized (Q3 2000–Q2 2003)

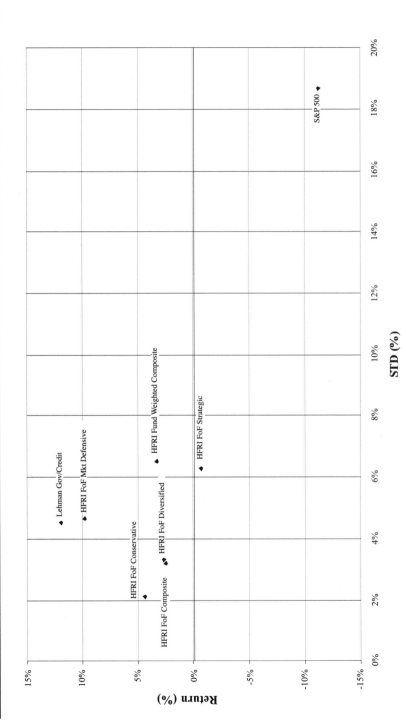

**HFRI Fund of Fund Indices Risk Return Comparison
3 Year Annualized (Q3 2000–Q2 2003)**

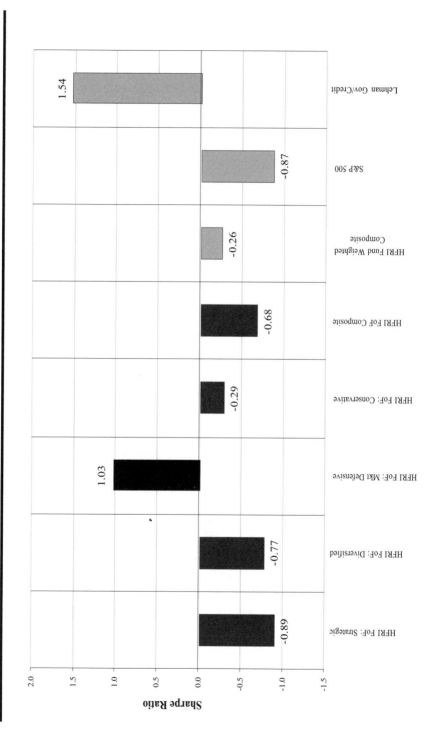

**HFRI Fund of Fund Indices Sharpe Ratio
3 Year Annualized (Q3 2000–Q2 2003)**

HFRI Fund of Fund Indices % of Positive Monthly Performance 3 Year (Q3 2000–Q2 2003)

Index	% Winning Months
HFRI FoF: Strategic	52.8%
HFRI FoF: Diversified	63.9%
HFRI FoF: Mkt Defensive	75.0%
HFRI FoF: Conservative	72.2%
HFRI FoF Composite	58.3%
HFRI Fund Weighted Composite	61.1%
S&P 500	44.4%
Lehman Gov/Credit	77.8%

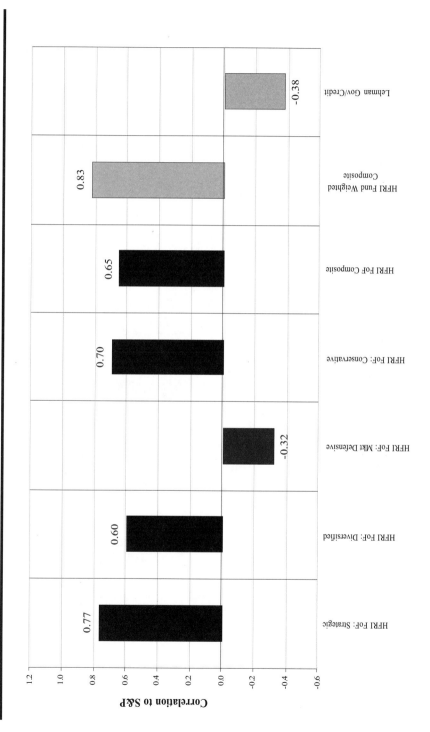

HFRI Fund of Fund Indices Correlation to S&P 500 Index 3 Year (Q3 2000–Q2 2003)

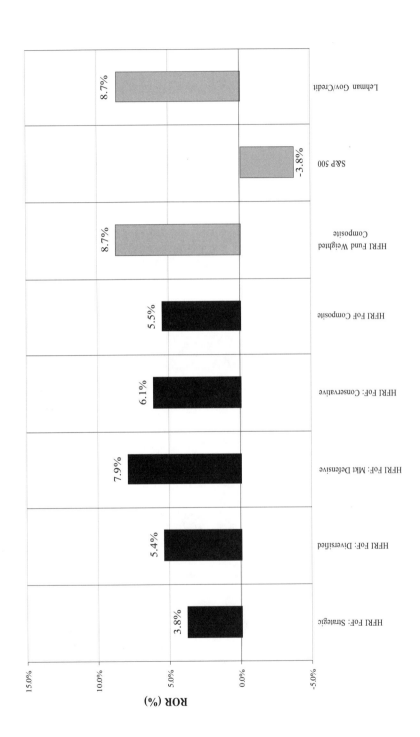

**HFRI Fund of Fund Indices Performance
5 Year Annualized (Q3 1998–Q2 2003)**

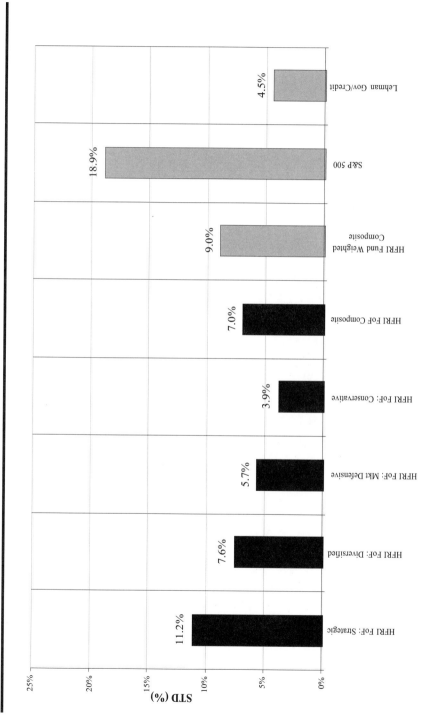

**HFRI Fund of Fund Indices Standard Deviation
5 Year Annualized (Q3 1998–Q2 2003)**

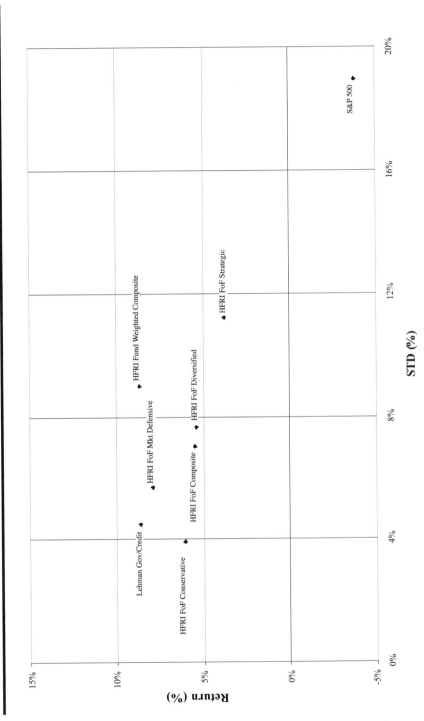

**HFRI Fund of Fund Indices Risk Return Comparison
5 Year Annualized (Q3 1998–Q2 2003)**

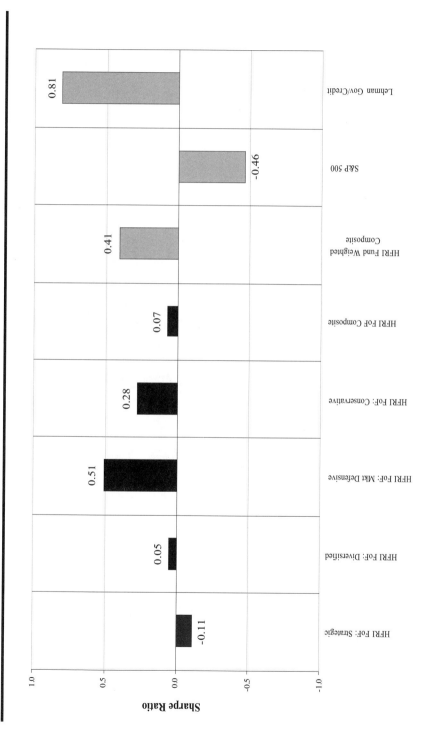

HFRI Fund of Fund Indices Sharpe Ratio
5 Year Annualized (Q3 1998–Q2 2003)

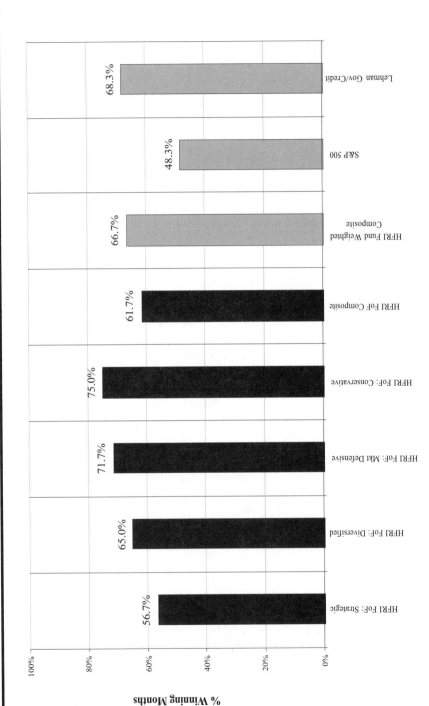

HFRI Fund of Fund Indices % of Positive Monthly Performance
5 Year (Q3 1998–Q2 2003)

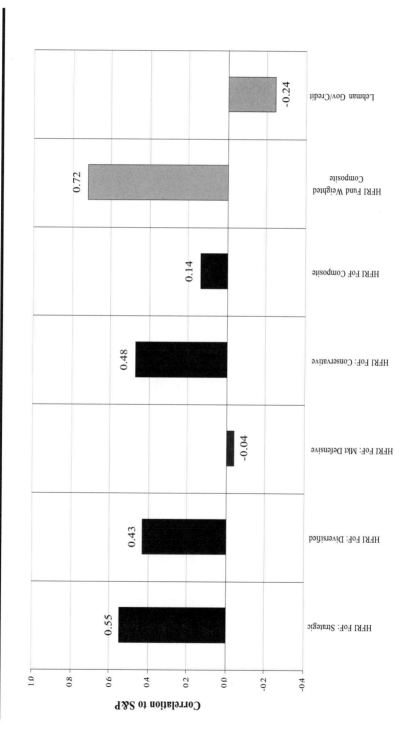

HFRI Fund of Fund Indices Correlation to S&P 500 Index
5 Year (Q3 1998–Q2 2003)

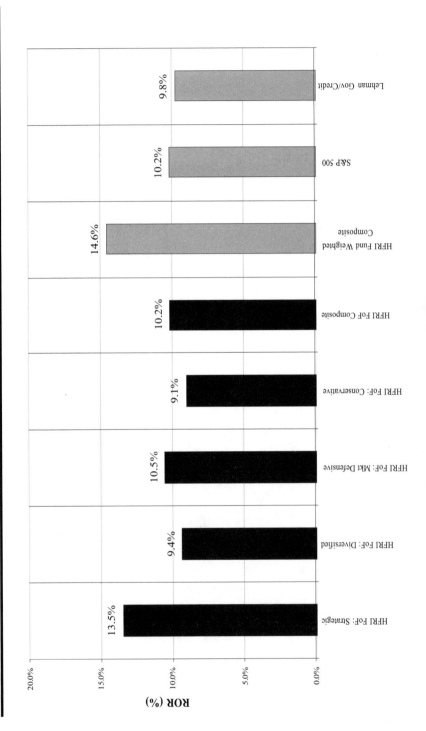

HFRI Fund of Fund Indices Performance Annualized Since Inception (1990–Q2 2003)

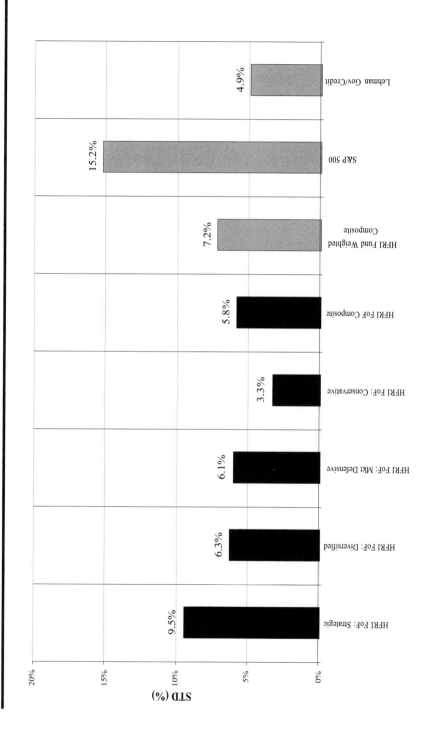

HFRI Fund of Fund Indices Standard Deviation Annualized Since Inception (1990–Q2 2003)

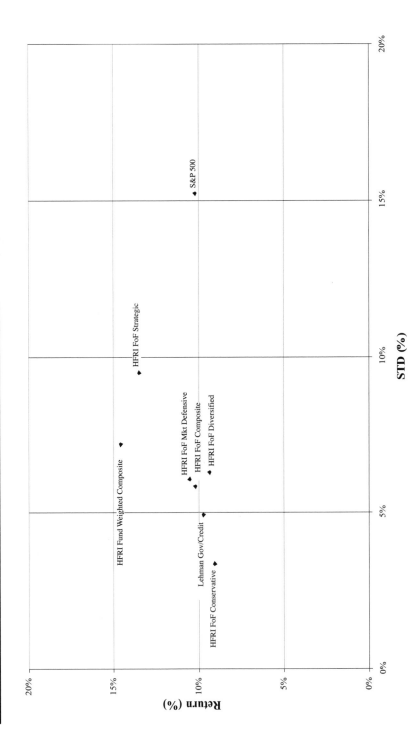

HFRI Fund of Fund Indices Risk Return Comparison Annualized Since Inception (1990–Q2 2003)

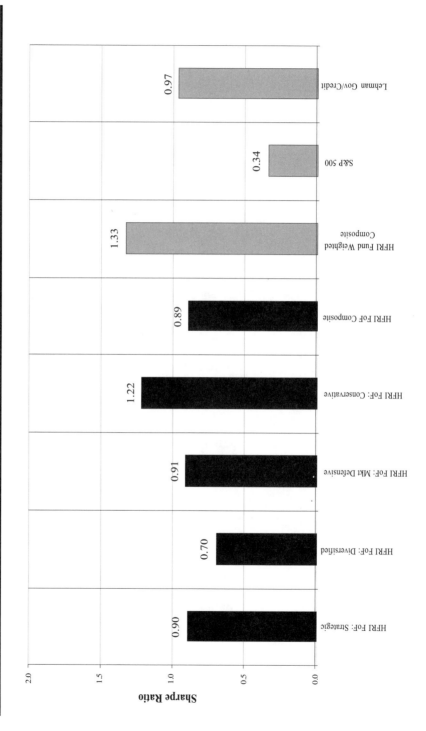

HFRI Fund of Fund Indices Sharpe Ratio
Since Inception (1990–Q2 2003)

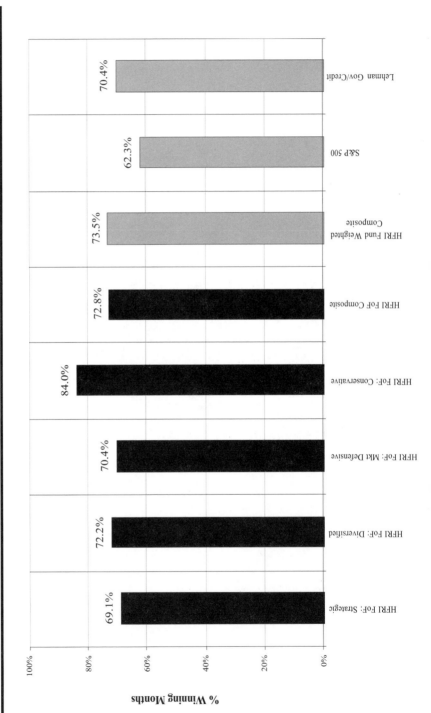

HFRI Fund of Fund Indices % of Positive Monthly Performance Since Inception (1990–Q2 2003)

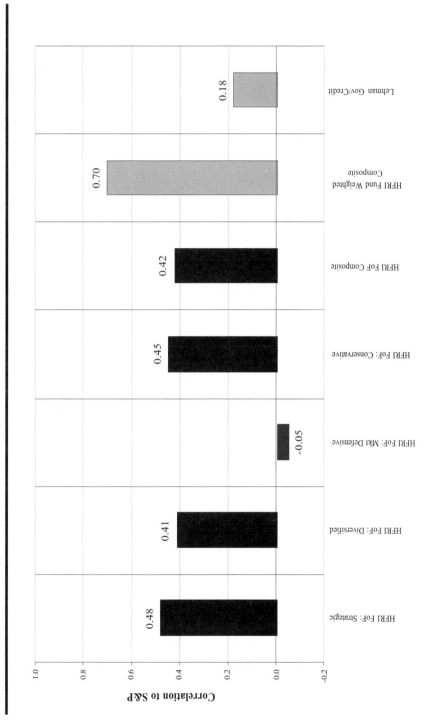

HFRI Fund of Fund Indices Correlation to S&P 500 Index Since Inception (1990–Q2 2003)

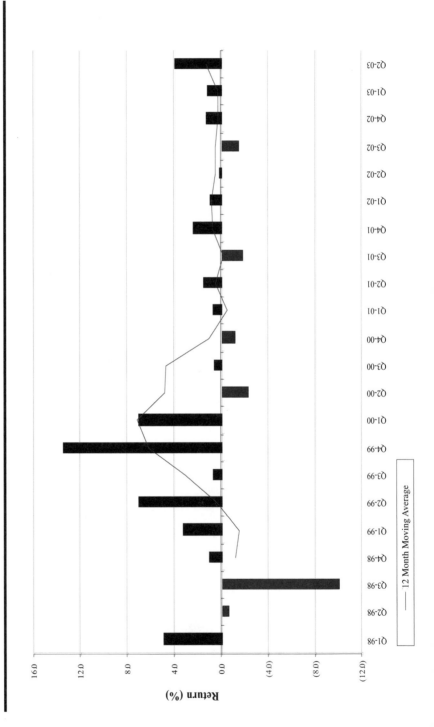

HFRI Fund of Funds Composite Index
Quarterly Performance 1998–Q2 2003

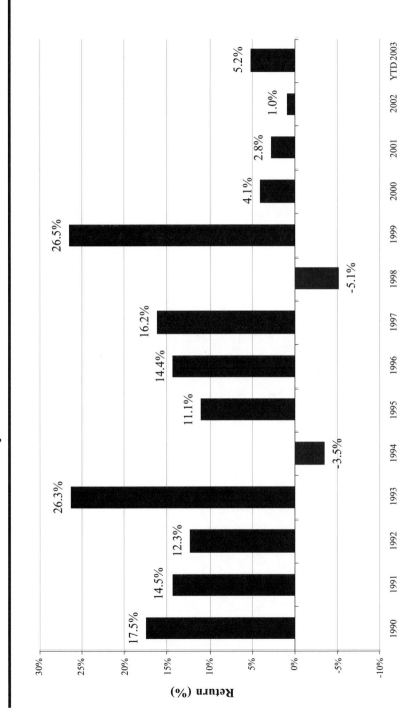

**HFRI Fund of Funds Composite Index
Yearly Performance 1990–YTD 2003**

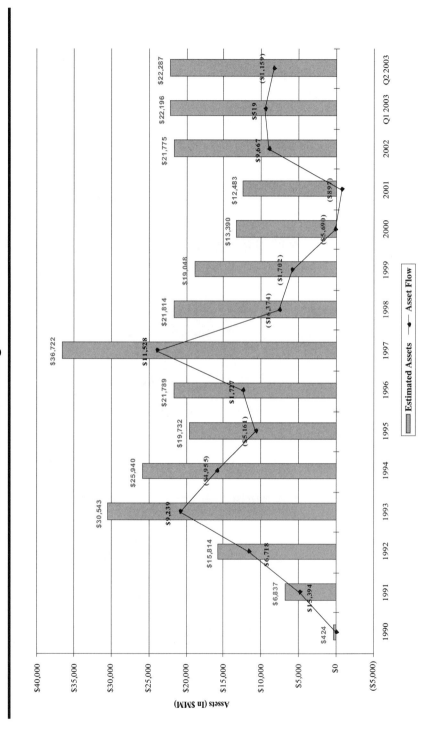

Estimated Growth of Assets/Asset Flow
HFRI Fund of Funds: Strategic Index 1990–Q2 2003

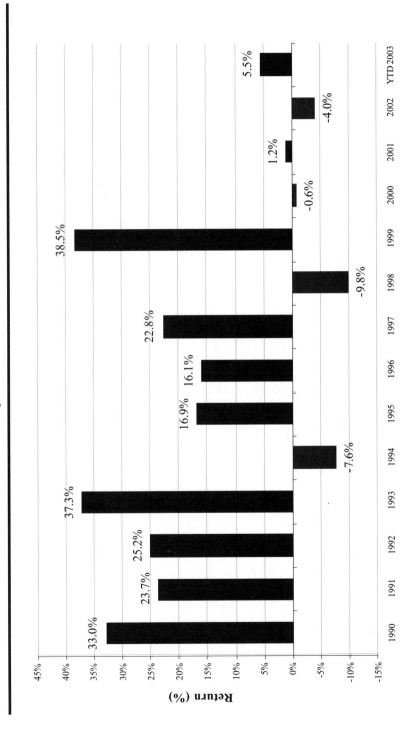

HFRI Fund of Funds: Strategic Index
Annualized Yearly Performance 1990–YTD 2003

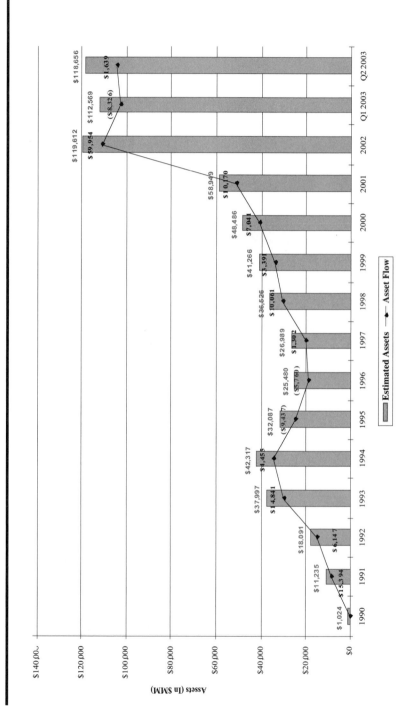

Estimated Growth of Assets/Asset Flow
HFRI Fund of Funds: Diversified Index 1990–Q2 2003

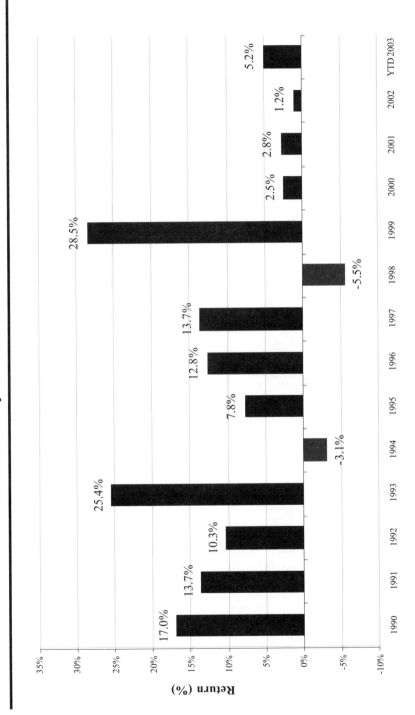

HFRI Fund of Funds: Diversified Index
Annualized Yearly Performance 1990–YTD 2003

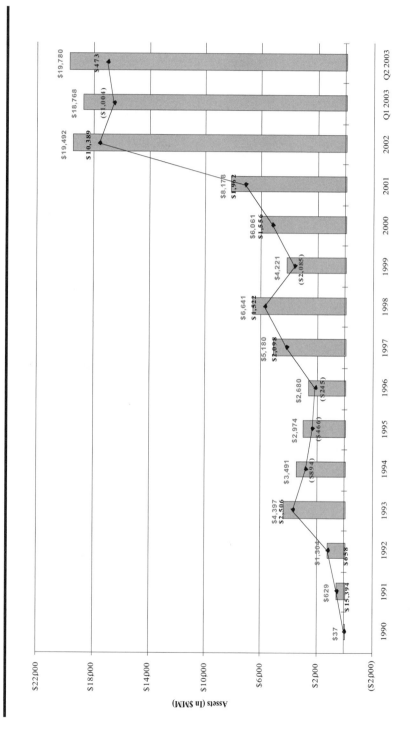

Estimated Growth of Assets/Asset Flow
HFRI Fund of Funds: Market Defensive Index 1990–Q2 2003

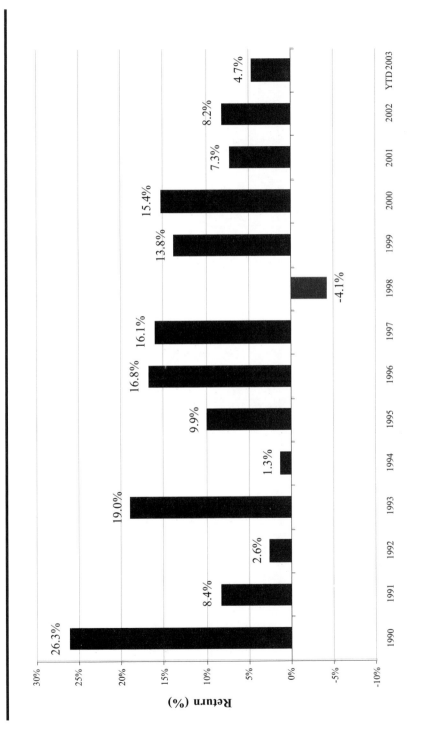

**HFRI Fund of Funds: Market Defensive Index
Annualized Yearly Performance 1990–YTD 2003**

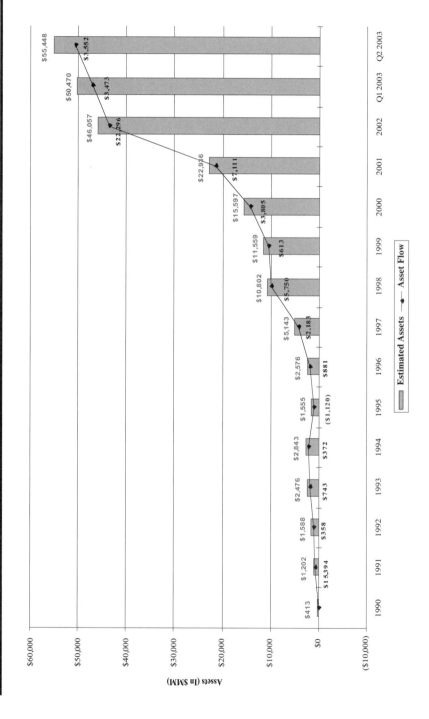

Estimated Growth of Assets/Asset Flow
HFRI Fund of Funds: Conservative Index 1990–Q2 2003

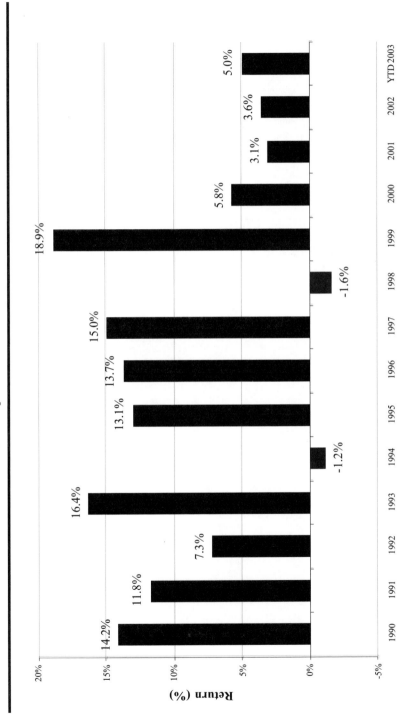

**HFRI Fund of Funds: Conservative Index
Annualized Yearly Performance 1990–YTD 2003**

Index

About Bloomberg

Bloomberg L.P., founded in 1981, is a global information services, news, and media company. Headquartered in New York, the company has nine sales offices, two data centers, and 87 news bureaus worldwide.

Bloomberg, serving customers in 126 countries around the world, holds a unique position within the financial services industry by providing an unparalleled range of features in a single package known as the BLOOMBERG PROFESSIONAL™ service. By addressing the demand for investment performance and efficiency through an exceptional combination of information, analytic, electronic trading, and Straight Through Processing tools, Bloomberg has built a worldwide customer base of corporations, issuers, financial intermediaries, and institutional investors.

BLOOMBERG NEWS®, founded in 1990, provides stories and columns on business, general news, politics, and sports to leading newspapers and magazines throughout the world. BLOOMBERG TELEVISION®, a 24-hour business and financial news network, is produced and distributed globally in seven different languages. BLOOMBERG RADIO℠ is an international radio network anchored by flagship station BLOOMBERG® 1130 (WBBR-AM) in New York.

In addition to the BLOOMBERG PRESS® line of books, Bloomberg publishes *BLOOMBERG MARKETS*™ and *BLOOMBERG WEALTH MANAGER*®. To learn more about Bloomberg, call a sales representative at:

Frankfurt:	49-69-92041-0	São Paulo:	5511-3048-4500
Hong Kong:	852-2977-6000	Singapore:	65-6212-1000
London:	44-20-7330-7500	Sydney:	61-2-9777-8600
New York:	1-212-318-2000	Tokyo:	81-3-3201-8900
San Francisco:	1-415-318-2960		

About the Author

Joseph G. Nicholas, J.D., is a leading authority on hedge funds, funds of funds, and alternative investment strategies. As founder and Chairman of HFR Group L.L.C. and its affiliated companies, Mr. Nicholas pioneered the areas of hedge fund transparency and indexation. The HFR companies specialize in alternative investments, providing investment products and advisory and research services. HFR Group includes HFR Asset Management, L.L.C., an SEC Registered Investment Adviser based in Chicago, specializing in fund of funds, index funds, product structuring, trading manager selection and risk management; HFR Europe, Ltd., a fund of funds and portfolio management company, with offices in Milan and London; and Hedge Fund Research, Inc., the industry's leading supplier of data and research on hedge funds, specializing in the construction and management of hedge fund indices. In addition to *Hedge Fund of Funds Investing*, Mr. Nicholas is author of *Market-Neutral Investing* (Bloomberg Press, 2000) and *Investing in Hedge Funds* (Bloomberg Press, 1999), among other writings. He is a frequent lecturer on topics relating to alternative investments and has appeared on CNN and *Nightly Business Report*. Mr. Nicholas received a Bachelor of Science degree in commerce from DePaul University and a Juris Doctor degree from the Northwestern University School of Law.

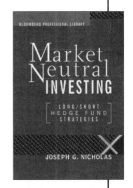